AT THE END OF THE AGES...

(The Abolition of Hell)

By

Bob Evely

D1445793

Additional copies of this book can be purchased at
www.graceevangel.org

Drop us a note at bob@graceevangel.org to receive
periodic free newsletters.

ISBN: 1-4107-1258-3 (e-book)
ISBN: 1-4107-1259-1 (Paperback)

This book is printed on acid free paper.

Scripture quotations noted from the NIV (New International
Version of the Bible), copyright 1973, 1978, 1984 by
International Bible Society.

DEDICATION

This book is lovingly dedicated to JILL...

My precious wife of 27 years, and the love of my life!

Who has walked with me; explored with me, laughed with me, cried with me,
grown with me, made mistakes with me;

But most importantly, has always "walked this road" with me.

ACKNOWLEDGMENTS

I begin my thanking my wonderful wife Jill, who has always been so supportive of my every endeavor. The writing of this book was no exception. Her encouragement has meant so much to me through the long process of writing, and her faithfulness in proof reading and offering suggestions was a tremendous help.

I also want to express appreciation for my late grandfather, Lewis Evely, who died in 1971 when I was still in high school. Many of his books were passed down to me, and were most helpful in my quest for the truth found in God's Word. My grandfather was a lay preacher, and taught the truth of the ultimate salvation of all as revealed in God's Word. I wish I had been further down this path while he was still alive.

I thank my parents, Paul & Ottolyn Evely, who have always encouraged me in the faith, and who continue to support me in so many ways.

I also thank Jill's parents, the late Dr. Howard R. Maynard (whom we miss so very much) and Bettie M. Maynard. They, too, have been nothing but supportive, and truly like a second set of parents. It is because of them that I could never understand the humor in the many "in-law" jokes and criticisms which have become all too common in this world.

I thank my children, of whom I am so very proud, including my two wonderful daughters-in-law whom I love as my own children. To Cris & Jen, Dusty & Sharon, Chad, Kari and Scott; I thank you for your love and support, and for your willingness to study the Scriptures and to think for yourself. I thank you all for being open to considering the doctrine of the ultimate salvation of all, as expressed in the Word of God. What I am most happy about is that none of you have accepted my beliefs simply because I am your father, but ALL of you have been open to hearing me out and exploring for yourselves. Special thanks to Chad for his laborious proof reading and corrections.

I thank those within our Tuesday evening Bible study, who may or may not agree with my viewpoints but who have been willing to listen, study, discuss, and be open to the possibility of the ultimate salvation of all.

Most certainly I thank our Heavenly Father for His love and His grace that is greater than anything mere mortals can understand; and the Lord Jesus Christ for making the ultimate sacrifice, to make our undeserved salvation possible.

Finally I thank you, the reader, for being willing to hear what I have to say, and to think for yourself. May God bless you in your quest for understanding as to the will and the ways of God.

Most Sincerely,

Bob Evely
Wilmore, KY (2002)

TABLE OF CONTENTS

INTRODUCTION

I believe that the Bible is the Word of God; perfect to the very word. We can learn some things about God by simply observing the universe, since God is the creator of all things. But when it comes to knowing details about God, and about His will and His purposes, we can only know those things that God has chosen to reveal to us.

After observing the evidence I have come to the firm conclusion that the Bible is God's revelation to mankind. Some claim that other writings are from God (Koran, Book of Mormon, etc), but I believe the evidence points clearly to the Bible as having sole claim to this status. It is important to know the evidence and to consider it for yourself. Many who believe that the Bible is the Word of God (or that the Koran is the Word of God) base their belief on the fact that their family or their teachers say that it is so. People who wave their Bibles in the air as they loudly proclaim, "This is the Word of God," don't really even know the evidence that supports this claim. Theirs is simply an emotional belief.

Having told you of my total confidence that the Bible is the Word of God, I go on to say with firm conviction that the Bible tells us of a time, at the end of the ages, when God will save **ALL** of mankind. The lake of fire (some call it hell) will be abolished, having accomplished its purpose.

Speculation? Heresy? Not at all! The abolition of hell is clearly taught in the Bible. The problem is that through the years the translations of the Bible have been "indoctrinated" with the biases of the men and women who translate it for us. As we will see in this study, the error began in the 5th century when "The Church" gave certain *opinions* the weight of church law. Men who taught otherwise were persecuted, and even killed. Their writings were burned. But was "The Church" correct? I have observed from church history that those leading "The Church" in the 5th century were unfamiliar with

Greek, which was the language of the original New Testament, and they were motivated by power and jealousy. "The Church" determined that the average person was not able to understand scripture, so the leaders kept the Bible to themselves. They did not want it to be translated into the language of the common man. The church leaders were the interpreters, teachers, and dispensers of truth.

I once thought that the English translations I used were perfect. But as I used different translations from time to time, I could see there were differences even between the translations; sometimes significant differences. Was the Bible the perfect, infallible Word of God, or not?

I observed the many arguments and disagreements that take place between churches, and even within churches. Most of these arguments result from differences in the interpretation of the Bible. Is there a way to really know truth?

As time went on I began to see the root of the problem. We have disagreements in doctrine not because the Bible is imperfect, but because:

    a.   The **translations** we use today are imperfect, and
    b.   The teachings of mankind (even the "experts") are imperfect, including the **interpretations** of what the Bible is teaching.

The Bible, in its pure form, is perfect. Translators, interpreters, teachers, preachers, scholars and theologians are imperfect.

I attended Asbury Theological Seminary in Wilmore, Kentucky. This is a "Wesleyan" school, which means that the basic teachings of John Wesley are accepted as being correct. Jesus Christ died for the sake of all, not just "the elect." Men have free will to make decisions, they are not predestined.

In a few of my classes I would hear a professor criticize the teachings of another seminary in Dallas that teaches predestination, and salvation only for "the elect." I know that both of these seminaries base their beliefs on the Bible, and both believe they are correct. But at least one of them must be wrong, and perhaps both are.

When I was first led to a firm belief in the ultimate salvation of all mankind, a friend advised that I should go and talk with a professor to get straightened around. Which professor? How can I know which professor is right, and which is wrong?

Living in Wilmore, Kentucky, one block from Asbury Theological Seminary, I hear this solution offered quite often. Whenever someone thinks that a person is in error in their beliefs, they are advised to go and talk with a seminary professor.

We are back to the days preceding the Reformation. If you have a question you ask the professor, the guardian of truth for "The Church." But the error that was expounded by "The Church" is what prompted the Reformation, to recover the truth that salvation is found solely in the grace of God, through faith.

The Reformation was a rebellion against "The Church" which had suppressed the truth and had led the average person into error.

A Reformation is needed again today, because we are in the same situation.

"The Church" has developed certain creeds, articles of religion, membership vows, and other mechanisms to tell people what truth is. One cannot simply turn to the Word of God to know truth. One must agree to, and sometimes sign, documents to ensure that certain beliefs are upheld. But these documents are not the Word of God; they are only man's opinions as to what the Word of God teaches. They are all different. At least some of them must be incorrect.

The purpose of this work is to help you to see that our thinking about God is trapped in bias and error. We believe things because we have been taught to believe them, and because we trust the teachers, professors and leaders of "The Church."

I have come to the firm conclusion that these teachings are wrong on many points. Modern Bible translations that are more interested in being "inclusive" and easy to read, lead us into error.

But if this is so, is there a way to know what God's Word really says? Is there a way to eliminate the bias and error of the translators? If the learned professors and teachers of our day have reached wrong conclusions, how can an average person like me know the truth?

This must be exactly what the people said in Jesus' day. Jesus, a simple carpenter, was teaching things that were very different from what the Pharisees, Scribes, professors and teachers of His day were saying. Small wonder that many could not break away from the teachings of the learned and respected Pharisees. It seems that we can't either!

I will not ask you to believe things that are contrary to what you have been taught, just because I believe them. I simply ask that you review certain evidences and facts with me, and keep your mind open. When I first began to talk openly about these things, a friend wanted to debate me, scripture against scripture. The problem was that every time I made a point, he would not even listen to my perspective. From the outset his determination was made. The prevailing church doctrine (as taught in Wesleyan circles) was correct, and I was wrong. The debate was not truly an objective study of scripture passages. Instead it was simply a one-sided hammering away in favor of a position that had already been reached.

There must be openness. If you close your mind and think that there is no possible way your Bible translation or your church doctrine can be in error, you might as well stop reading right now.

This is not intended to be a scholarly work on the subject. If you want a scholarly work, I can recommend many, starting with those listed in the final chapter. But don't read any of these until you finish this book. Many who have started reading the scholarly works favoring "Universalism" get so bogged down with the details that they give up. They end up thinking there is no way they can ever understand, so they quit searching.

No, this is not a scholarly work. But the basic points are very simple. That's why I saw a need to write this book. My intention is to show you the basics, which are more than enough to display God's plan to ultimately save all of mankind. You can read the scholarly works later.

You may already be questioning how God could possibly save all of mankind as you bring to mind all of the familiar passages making mention of an eternal torment. These passages will not be ignored. Remember, this is coming from one who believes 100% that the Bible is the perfect, infallible Word of God.

I grew up in the church (mostly Methodist). At the age of 40 I moved to Wilmore, Kentucky to attend Asbury Theological Seminary where I earned my M.Div. (Master of Divinity) degree. I served as a bi-vocational pastor for 8-1/2 years. The last church I served was very difficult to leave. All five of my children and my two wonderful daughters-in-law were a part of this church family. My daughter was the Worship Leader. Two of my sons were a part of the "worship team," as I was myself. I loved preaching. I loved teaching. I loved my church family. I was comfortable.

But when I became convinced of God's wonderful, amazing, miraculous plan to save all mankind at the end of the ages, I was forced to give up my comfortable position. I knew it would be wrong for me to teach things which clearly contradicted the doctrine of the church I served, as it would lead to arguments and division. It would also be wrong for me to suppress these things I have found to be true, and to go along with the falsehoods being taught by "The Church." As difficult as it was, I stepped down as pastor in May 2002 to focus on writing, teaching, and leading a "church" where proclaiming the truth of universal reconciliation would not cause division.

Having provided these opening thoughts, I ask you to read on, and THINK! I will repeat this often...*THINK FOR YOURSELF!*

Challenge the biases that have influenced you, and that continue to influence you. Keep your mind open. Be a bit skeptical of what I have to say; that is OK! No one should allow himself to be led astray! But consider the possibility of a God whose grace is even greater than you have ever before imagined!

ABBREVIATIONS USED

The following abbreviations are used throughout when referring to various Bible translations.

CLNT – Concordant Literal New Testament
CVOT – Concordant Version of the Old Testament
NIV – New International Version
KJV – King James Version

Where not specifically noted, the CLNT is used for New Testament references, and the CVOT for Old Testament references.

REFERENCES

In the text I will note just the title and author of works being referenced. You can refer to the final chapter, "Recommended Reading" for complete information on each reference.

EXPLANATORY NOTES

The reader may wonder why I have used quotation marks when referring to "The Church" or "The Gospel."

In our modern Bible translations "Church" comes from the Greek "ecclesia," which literally means "called-out-ones." Here again our beliefs have been shaped by the translators. In a few cases "ecclesia" is used but cannot possibly refer to "The Church," since it refers to an angry mob, or a courtroom jury. In these cases the translator uses another word instead of "church." But these cases show us that when God uses the word "ecclesia" He does not always mean the same thing. "Ecclesia" is simply a group of people "called out" for a particular purpose. A complete study of the ramifications of this would be a book in itself. Suffice it to say that "The Church" has taken on a form through history and tradition which is not necessarily biblical. "The Church," as used in this work, refers to the organized, orthodox institution which is commonly referred to today as "church," as opposed to the "ecclesia" which is simply God's people (Believers) worldwide, regardless of which (if any) organized "church" they are a part of.

"The Gospel" is another greatly misunderstood word. The Concordant Version does not use the word "gospel" but simply preserves the Greek "evangel" which should be easy to understand (since we use the words "evangelism" and "evangelist" every day). A complete study of "evangel" would be a book in itself. The basic problem, simply stated, is that the Bible translators have shaped for us what "The Gospel" is. But "evangel" simply means "good news," and it is not always the same. When we read about "The Gospel" that John the Baptist proclaimed we have been taught that it is the same "Gospel" that Paul proclaimed. But "evangel" can mean different things in different instances, since the word simply means "good news." I have come to see a big difference in how God has worked in various ages, and there is a big difference between the "evangel of the kingdom" when the kingdom was being introduced, and the "evangel of grace" which Paul says is simply: "Be reconciled."

When the word "orthodox" is used, it does not mean "truth" as opposed to "falsehood." Orthodox means that which is commonly believed to be truth by the *majority* of "The Church," as opposed to a dissenting view. Which position is actually truth is another matter.

"Universalism" as used in this work is a belief in the ultimate salvation of **ALL** at the end of the ages, based on the Word of God. The term is to be differentiated from those who may proclaim a universal salvation without any biblical foundation, or from any particular "denomination" which may contain the word "Universalist." "Universalism" as used in this work does not deny the reality of God's judgment or the lake of fire. It does not condone sin, and it does not eliminate or minimize the need for Christ's work upon the cross.

"Universalism" as used in this work is synonymous with "universal reconciliation", "universal salvation", "the restitution of all things", or "the ultimate salvation of all."

Chapter One

THE BIBLE: HAS GOD SPOKEN TO US?

This is an important question, and a crucial starting point for our considerations. Is the Bible really God's Word as many claim? That is to say, is the Bible really God speaking to mankind, or is it just a collection of the writings of men?

If the Bible is not the Word of God there is little reason to continue the discussion that follows. Why turn to the Bible to find answers to our questions? We can instead use our morals, reason and imagination to determine what God must be like, what is right and what is wrong, and what lies ahead for us after this life has ended. Or if the Bible is not a message from God to us, perhaps we can just never know about these things.

REVELATION

It is true that we can learn some things about God from sources other than the Bible. God's physical creation can be explored and examined. In this world we see beauty indicative of a very creative God. We see order and precision that points to a very intelligent God. We see within our conscience the fingerprint of a moral God. But from these sources we can only learn so much about the God who created this universe.

But what if God **wants** us to know more about Him? What if He wants us to know the things He approves of, or the things He does not approve of? What if He wants to tell us things about the future? What if He wants to give us assurances about what will happen after we die?

If God wanted to accomplish these things, He could only do so by **revealing** things about Himself. Could the Bible be this revelation? Could it be a communication from God Himself to humanity, to tell us things He wants us to know? Could it be intended to give us direction and counsel in this uncertain age?

WHAT IS THE EVIDENCE?

My purpose in this work is not to examine all of the evidence that the Bible is the Word of God. This would be an entire book in itself. I recommend "The New Evidence That Demands a Verdict" by Josh McDowell, an excellent source of information along these lines.

But since the reader must be assured of the inspiration of the Bible in order to appreciate the discussions which follow, let us take a few minutes to list the basic evidence that the Bible is, in fact, from God.

1. There is great continuity found in the Bible, despite the fact that it was written over a period of some 1500 years through some 40 different authors. A divine unity seems to prevail, perhaps because it was the single holy spirit of God which was actually at work.

2. In the book "God's Eonian Purpose" by Adlai Loudy we read that the Bible displays "a divine order and progress in the unfolding of truth." (page 22) This order points to a divine creator, much as the world and universe in which we live point to an intelligent and divine creator.

3. There are billions of copies of the Bible in circulation; more than any other book in history. Furthermore, the Bible has been translated into some 2200 different languages. Could it be that humanity recognizes the divine nature of the Bible, thereby leading to such widespread proliferation?

4. There is more manuscript evidence to support the Bible than any ten pieces of classical literature combined.

5. The Bible has survived through the ages despite many attempts to eradicate it from the face of the earth.

6. Historical events noted in the Bible have been repeatedly supported by other historical accounts and archeological finds.

7. Many of the prophecies contained within the Bible have been fulfilled to the minutest detail. These fulfillments are supported by historical accounts and archeological finds. This lends credence to the other prophecies found in the Bible that continue to await fulfillment.

8. There is no "whitewashing" found in the Bible which is typical in most other histories written by men. King David, for example, is presented as a man after God's own heart, yet his sins and imperfections are revealed alongside his greatness.

9. Historical accounts show us that the scribes who copied the holy scriptures, preserving it through the ages, took great pains to ensure complete accuracy. They were motivated by the firm belief that these writings were truly from the hand of God.

10. In the Bible we find God **revealing** Himself to mankind, not mankind speculating or reasoning **about** God as we find in other "holy" writings.

Some may question why some writings were included in the Bible while others were rejected. They may argue that this human element was imperfect, and therefore the writings selected for inclusion in the Bible may have been chosen incorrectly. History shows us, though, that the Believers in the years immediately following the demise of the apostles took great pains to determine which writings were truly inspired by God, and which were not. One might say that men did not **choose** the writings to be included in the Bible, but they simply **discovered** or **discerned** which writings were inspired by God.

The early Believers examined the manuscripts and asked:

1. Was this written by a true prophet of God?
2. Were the contents confirmed by the acts of God?
3. Were the writings accepted by the people of God?
   The bottom line...are these writings divinely inspired?

Again, the reader is strongly encouraged to consult "The New Evidence That Demands a Verdict" by Josh McDowell. We should know the evidence for our beliefs, both to strengthen our own faith and to enable us to energetically share that faith with others.

The Bible **IS** the Word of God. This is not just a statement made from a blind faith. It is not just choosing sides as one would choose a favorite football team. It is not basing a decision on emotion, or because one was raised within a certain framework of belief. This is a most important question...Is the Bible the Word of God? Examine the evidence, and know **why** you believe.

IS GOD'S WORD PERFECT?

Now let us move on to the next point...If the Bible is really God's revelation to mankind, would He allow it to become distorted so as to confuse His message? If this is man's writing, it may be fallible because it is derived from the fallible reasoning and perspective of man. If this is God's writing, it is coming from the **perfect** reasoning and perspective of God.

Since God used man as His instrument, and since man is imperfect, one may argue that while God may have revealed Himself to us in this manner, the resultant message from God is imperfect. But again, if the Bible is God's intent to communicate His will to mankind, why would He allow corruption and imperfection to cloud the message and cause confusion?

On page 147 of "The Greek Elements," published by Concordant Publishing Concern, we find the following comment on the issue at hand.

> *"Since God is the real Author of the Scriptures, the language is refined and exact beyond the power of human appreciation. While He uses human words, He does not use them with human laxity. Their meaning is to be gathered from His own usage, rather than from the writings of men who use words loosely and inaccurately, or from philosophic literature devoted to human speculations. To a surprising extent the sacred book is self-sufficient, and he who knows all that it contains will have little recourse to external sources of information. These have their place and value, but their evidence is far inferior to a microscopic examination of the living Word of God itself."*

In 2 Peter 1:21 we are told that prophecy was not carried on by the will of man, but "being carried on by holy spirit, holy men of God speak." (CLNT)

God's holy spirit thus spoke through men…it was not left to the men to speak for themselves, trying to relay what God had told them. The very words of these men were, then, inspired by God Himself.

In "God's Eonian Purpose" by Adlai Loudy we read:

> *"Thought can only be expressed in words, and those words must express the exact thought of the speaker, otherwise, his exact thought is not expressed." (page 24)*

If God, then, wished to reveal His thoughts to mankind, how could He have done so if the corrupted and imperfect thoughts of men were permitted to creep into the revelation? How could we ever make a determination as to exactly what God meant, and what was simply a distortion attributed to the imperfection of men?

5

If God wanted His revealed thoughts and His will to be transmitted to mankind in perfection, He would simply cause each word to be inspired. He would give the men He had chosen the very words He wanted them to use, thus preserving the exact thoughts He was wishing to relay. These men would not, then, write as **they** desired or as **they** determined, but instead they would be instruments used by God to record the very words **God** had chosen.

Not only are these logical assumptions to make as we consider how God would preserve His thoughts for mankind, but the perfection of God's Word is also supported by the very precision we find when studying it. As we will see in later chapters, this precision and perfection has been clouded by the carelessness and tradition-bias found in our English translations, but if we can get back to the original languages we will come to appreciate the perfection of every word.

Some will argue against the perfection of the Bible, citing inconsistencies or difficulties. Unfortunately there are many who misapply or misinterpret the Bible, making it appear that there are inconsistencies, or that the truth God presents may be beyond any human understanding. But the failures of those who incorrectly apply or interpret the Bible do not mean that the Bible itself is imperfect. This is another matter altogether. There are really two issues:

a. The perfection of every word found within the Bible, and
b. Accurately interpreting and applying the Word of God.

In this section we are considering the first point…the perfection of the writings themselves. Later in this work we will look at the second point…how are we to interpret and apply that which we find within the Bible?

We have come to understand, then, that the Bible is God's Word, and in the original languages it is perfect, word for word. Some may go further and claim that certain English translations are perfect (e.g. King James Version), but errors are clearly present in the translations of man. This becomes very clear when studying the Bible using several different translations. There are many differences, and some of these differences are significant.

Many translation errors can be attributed to the theological biases of the translators. Some passages may be difficult to translate, or the passages may seem to be inconsistent with the "orthodox" beliefs of the translator, so the translator relies upon his understanding of the ways of God and makes decisions relating to the passage being translated.

I am not wanting to destroy the reader's confidence in the Bible they are using. While errors are present, the central fact of salvation as offered by God to humanity is intact. However, further details concerning such things as Heaven, Hell, Judgment, The Church, The Kingdom, and many other topics get clouded by the inconsistent translations of men. Later in this work we will explore how we can overcome these difficulties.

WHAT ABOUT OTHER SOURCES CLAIMING TO BE GOD'S REVELATION?

Those who are a part of the Islamic faith would say that the Koran is the sacred work inspired by God. Mormons point to the Book of Mormon. Christian Scientists point to the works of Mary Baker Eddy. Likewise those of other faiths would point to their own "sacred writings" and say they are from the hand of God. How do we know that the Bible is from God, and these others are not?

We have presented a few of the evidences in support of the Bible, and we have directed the reader to the McDowell work for a more extensive study. These same evidences do not exist in support of any other supposedly divine work. The Bible is unique.

As to any writings that would claim to be a further word from God subsequent to the Bible, Colossians 1:25 tells us that Paul was granted the "administration of God" to "**complete** the word of God" (CLNT), thus closing the door on any who would lead us astray saying that they had a further revelation from God.

Furthermore, we note that in the Bible we see God speaking to mankind and **revealing** Himself to mankind. He uses men as His instruments, but it is God speaking directly to us. This is not so in other works where we see mankind speculating and speaking *about* "god."

THINK FOR YOURSELF!
Is the Bible really the perfect Word of God?

If it is not, you can read it if you want to, or you can spend your time reading other books, taking on hobbies, watching television, or doing whatever you like as you live your life. It doesn't matter what you do with the Bible if it is just a collection of the writings of men.

But if the Bible **is** the Word of God, we must read it, study it, understand it, properly apply it, and appreciate it for what it is…God revealing Himself to us. If the Bible is the Word of God, it is the most cherished key to life.

Do you believe the Bible is God's Word simply because your pastor said it was so? Do you believe because your parents have told you it is so? Do you believe because everyone takes sides, and you have chosen to side with those claiming the Bible is the Word of God? These may be good reasons for choosing your favorite football team or musical artist, but we are talking about something much more important, with far-reaching implications.

Is the Bible the Word of God? I have directed you to at least some of the evidence. Search for yourself. Think for yourself! Know **why** you believe!

Chapter Two

FINDING A RELIABLE TRANSLATION

It is a challenging experience today to buy a Bible. One walks into the Bible section of a bookstore and finds dozens of different translations, packaged a number of different ways in the form of "study Bibles" for every conceivable circumstance. How does one decide which Bible is the best?

In comparing the various translations available for any given Bible passage we find differences, yet we know the original contained the same Greek or Hebrew. Who made the decisions as to the correct English words to use? Which translation is correct?

Each translation was prepared by a person or group of persons who used their best judgment in relaying to us what the original Greek or Hebrew intended to say. As we study Scripture, we are placing our faith in the ability, faithfulness, and earnestness of the translators who did the work.

THE ULTIMATE TRANSLATION

It would be best for us to use a Greek New Testament and a Hebrew Old Testament as we study. Even here, though, there would be decisions to be made. In the world today we do not possess the original manuscript upon which Paul wrote his epistles, or upon which the four gospel accounts were recorded. Instead we have many "manuscripts" which have been preserved, some of which may contain an entire book of the Bible and others which may contain only fragments.

9

There are differences in the manuscripts that have survived to this day. As we examine them all, decisions must be made as to which is closest to the single original manuscript. This is not our purpose here. Suffice it to say; many have dedicated a large part of their lives to examining the manuscripts and making these decisions. They sometimes disagree. As a result, you will find a few verses in the King James Version that are not present in the New International Version, because different Greek or Hebrew texts were used. (See Acts 28:29 as an example.) Nothing major is changed, and they are very close, but they are not identical.

I refer you to "God's Eonian Purpose" by Adlai Loudy (see listing in the final chapter) for a discussion of how it was determined which manuscripts are the most reliable. You can find many similar discussions by other authors as well.

Once we have made our decisions as to the most reliable manuscripts, we will have our Greek New Testament and Hebrew Old Testament, and we can begin. But while this is the ideal, it would be unreasonable to think that every earnest seeker will dedicate him/herself to a study of Greek and Hebrew.

DIFFERENT TRANSLATIONS

As we will see in later chapters, the biases of the translators have crept into the translation. A single Greek word will be translated using several different English words, sometimes with drastically different meanings. The translator has certain theological beliefs going into the translation effort. He cannot prevent these beliefs from entering into his work.

Through the years I have drifted from one translation to another. I began with the New International Version, and drifted to the New American Standard Version and then to the New King James Version, seeking the one that was closest to the original languages. Some prefer the newer, easier to read translations. For some purposes these have value, but I have come to value a translation that is closer to the original writings over one that is simply easier to read. In making the translation easier to read, someone made decisions on my behalf as they provided the English rendering, and I'm not sure I trust their judgments.

If we wish to study the truth that God has chosen to reveal to mankind, we will need a consistent, carefully developed, unbiased translation. Most modern translations are developed to be easier to read and understand. But these translations will only allow us to know the translator's viewpoint, and will not provide a clear, unbiased look at God's Word itself.

For the person who is earnestly seeking the pure, word for word rendering of the Bible, closest to the original languages, I recommend the Concordant Literal New Testament (CLNT) and the Concordant Version of the Old Testament (CVOT). The Concordant Version was prepared in such a way as to eliminate human bias, as much as is possible, and to seriously study and carefully conclude the meaning intended by God for each word used in the original manuscripts.

THE CONCORDANT VERSION

Only a few of the Old Testament books have been completed to date, although the remaining books are in progress. The Concordant Literal New Testament, however, was first published in 1926 by the Concordant Publishing Concern, then led by Mr. A. E. Knoch. It has been revised several times since its original publication.

Mr. Knoch and his associates went about their work very systematically. They wanted to study, and to allow others to study, the pure Word of God, untainted by the judgments of men as far as can be achieved.

The translation assumes that if God chose to use two distinct Greek words, He had a reason for doing so and it would behove the earnest student to seek the distinction God was wanting to make. Most current translations, for example, use the single word "love" when the Greek uses three distinct words. Current translations use the word "hell" to denote three different Greek words.

11

Even worse than this, most English translations will take a single word that God has chosen in the originals, and translate it in different ways to suit the idea the translator is wishing to relay, allowing his biases and preconceived notions to shape his translation. For example, God uses many times in the New Testament the single word "aion," yet this will sometimes be translated "eternal," sometimes "age," and sometimes "world." How can a **single** word used by God mean "eternal" in some cases, and something far more temporary in others?

Perhaps if the Bible is simply a collection of man's writings, such sloppiness in word usage could occur. In relaying his thoughts a man may sometimes use one word and sometimes another, without much thought or care as to any precision or distinction. But even in the case of men, if a distinct idea was being presented, great care would be taken in word selection so as not to lose the meaning of the thought being relayed. In the business world I have written many letters to customers or prospective customers. Where a crucial matter is at stake I choose my words very carefully, considering the precise impact upon the reader.

If the Bible is the revelation of God, and if He is desiring to reveal certain ideas to mankind, would He not take precise care in choosing His every word?

HOW THE CONCORDANT VERSION WAS DEVELOPED

In developing the Concordant Translation, the following method was used.

Every single Greek word was closely examined. Each word was studied in every occurrence within the New Testament to determine the best English equivalent to be used. As much as was possible the meaning for each word was determined from the way the word was used within the New Testament, and not how other human authors may have used the word.

To preserve distinctions made by God, each individual Greek word was matched with a unique English equivalent. The same English word was not used for different Greek words, and differing English words were not used when a single Greek word was used.

The translation was named "Concordant Literal" because of this methodology. Individual words were translated not because a human translator chose an English rendering which could vary from phrase to phrase based on his opinion. Instead, a "concordance" was employed to examine every instance where a single Greek word was used, and based on all of these readings a single English equivalent was determined. God had a reason for using the **same** Greek word in multiple cases, and He had a reason for using different Greek words as He intended to relay **distinct** meanings.

This word-for-word literal approach seems quite scientific and straightforward, but the fact of the matter is that the final product would be very difficult to use. In English we generally speak in terms of a subject (Dick), followed by a verb to indicate some action (threw), followed by an object upon which the verb acts (the ball). Not so with the Greek, which could be something closer to "threw the ball Dick." We know which is the subject and which is the object by the form of the word, usually the word ending.

Our word-for-word translation would thus be very difficult to read and study. Consider also that we have just looked at a very simple example (Dick threw the ball). Consider how the difficulty (threw the ball Dick) would be amplified when reading some of Paul's lengthy sentences.

And so the Concordant translation takes one final step in putting the translation into English "idiom." In doing so there may be times when a single Greek word could result in several different English words, but this is kept to a minimum, and any English words employed continue to retain the original single Greek **idea**. When God chooses a particular Greek (or Hebrew) word, He is intending to express a particular thought, but because of language differences it may be necessary to use a variety of English words to express this single thought. But in using these various English words, always the same Greek or Hebrew **thought** must be relayed.

In order to remain accountable to the reader, the Concordant translation provides everything that is needed to trace back to the original, so the English idiom is not totally relied-upon. As we read this translation, then, we are not required to accept the fact that "brotherly fondness" is the best translation in 1 Thessalonians 4:9. We can go to the "Greek-English Keyword Concordance" at the back of the Concordant Literal New Testament and find under "brotherly fondness."

Greek = philadelphia (FOND-brother-ness)

So the Greek in this case is "philadelphia," and the single English equivalent for this compound word is "FOND-brother-ness." Furthermore we see in the concordance other occurrences of the same Greek word, allowing us to trace its usage ourselves.

Unlike other English translations, the reader can examine for himself the English word used to translate any given word in the original Greek. While not perfect, the method used by the Concordant translation is scientific, systematic, uniform, and consistent.

"UNSEARCHABLE RICHES"
Besides publishing the Concordant Version, the Concordant Publishing Concern has also published continuously since 1909 a quarterly magazine entitled "Unsearchable Riches." As the Concordant Version was being developed and revised, many articles in "Unsearchable Riches" share with the reader the study and deliberation process. In developing this translation, great deliberation was invested in each word. Unlike any other translation, this entire process is open to the scrutiny of the Bible student.

"Unsearchable Riches" is still published today, and many (if not all) back issues, as well as a comprehensive index, is available from the Concordant Publishing Concern.

WHY IS THE CONCORDANT VERSION NOT BETTER KNOWN?

If the Concordant translation is as good as I have made it appear to be, why is it not better known, and why can't it be found in most Christian bookstores?

First, the Concordant translation is very literal, and therefore somewhat difficult to read. Unfortunately Bible translating has become very commercial, and since people seem more concerned with using a translation that is easy to read, they are not interested in a literal translation that is more difficult to read (even though it is more reliable). Book stores, even Bible book stores, tend to stock items that sell in greater quantities as this results in greater financial profit.

Second, the reader should be aware that using the Concordant translation will lead us to see certain theological points differently. You will find that some teachings as presented by most "orthodox" denominations of the current day are inaccurate, because we have allowed truth to become clouded and distorted by carelessness in handling God's Word. Today there is great pressure within the "orthodox church" to maintain the historic teachings of the denominations.

To illustrate this point, there is a problem when we translate the **single** Greek "aion" with very **different** English renderings, sometimes with the concept of "eternal" and other times with a less than eternal concept such as "world" or "age." This distinction that is made in the Greek is now lost in most current translations, causing much truth from God's revelation to be lost. We will see later in this work that a proper and consistent translation will change what we have come to accept as "eternal" punishment to "eonian" or "age-abiding" punishment.

Because an intense study of God's Word as concordantly rendered would result in some variances with the teachings of the "orthodox denominations" today, there is not overwhelming support from the

15

church for the Concordant Version, just as before Martin Luther initiated the "Reformation" against the Roman Catholic Church there was not overwhelming support for any version of the Bible besides the one sanctioned by "The Church." At that time the Roman Catholic Church wanted to remain in the position of "dispenser of the truth." The church did not want to leave it to the common man to read or study the Bible for himself. Furthermore, the church claimed that some of the alternative translations were contrary to the church's interpretation of the Bible, and contrary to many of the traditional teachings of the Catholic Church.

As a result of the Reformation we have learned that some of the church's teachings of that day were incorrect. Until there is another Reformation of sorts to point out the error of certain traditional "orthodox" teachings, there will be a suppression of certain truths.

Don't take my word for it! Examine the Concordant Literal New Testament to make your own decisions. In the remainder of this work I will give you some additional things to think about, and ask that you begin your own search for the truth. Don't assume what your church has taught or is teaching you is totally correct. Why do you believe the things you believe about God? Is it because your church has taught you these things? Is it because your pastor believes these things? Is it because your parents taught you these things since your childhood?

Paul commended the Bereans because they did not assume what Paul preached was correct. (Acts 17:11) Instead they examined the scriptures to be sure.

Read on. Think about these things. Examine the scriptures. Be diligent in your search. This is the very word of God we are considering!

FOR FURTHER STUDY

The Concordant Literal New Testament is difficult to find, since it does not have the commercial popularity to gain the interest of bookstores. You can purchase it directly from the publisher.

"The Concordant Literal New Testament With Keyword Concordance"
> *Concordant Publishing Concern*
> *15570 Knochaven Road, Santa Clarita, CA 91387*
> 661/252-2112 email@concordant.org
> www.concordant.org
> [The Concordant Literal New Testament is also available on CD ROM.]

"The Concordant Version of the Old Testament"
> *Concordant Publishing Concern*
> [Not entirely completed, but many of the individual books in the Old Testament can be purchased from the publisher.]

"Unsearchable Riches" – a bimonthly magazine
> *Concordant Publishing Concern*
> [A wonderful magazine filled with thought-provoking and well researched articles concerning the Word of God. All back issues are still available since the magazine was first published in 1909, and a topical and text index is also available from the publisher.]

I suggest visiting the Concordant website, where you will find many good publications.

Chapter Three

HOW LONG IS ETERNITY?

G. Campbell Morgan is one of the most well-known and respected Bible teachers and preachers in history. He worked as an associate of D. L. Moody in the Northfield Bible conferences, and he served as pastor of Westminster Chapel in London from 1904-1917 and again from 1933-1945. During his second term at Westminster Dr. D. Martyn Lloyd-Jones served as his associate.

Morgan has become known as the "Prince of Bible Expositors," and has written a host of well known and respected books. The primary focus of his ministry was the study and teaching of the Bible.

In his book "God's Methods With Men" (pages 185-6) Morgan says:

> "Let me say to Bible students that we must be very careful how we use the word 'eternity.' We have fallen into great error in our constant use of that word. There is no word in the whole Book of God corresponding with our 'eternal' which as commonly used among us means absolutely without end. The strongest Scripture word used with reference to the existence of God is—'unto the ages of the ages,' which does not literally mean eternally."

DON'T TAKE A MAN'S OPINION

Mr. Morgan was a serious student of the Bible, and he served within a very "orthodox" church setting, and he continues to this day to be highly respected by preachers and scholars; yet he tells us that when we read the word "eternity" in our modern English Bibles, it is not a correct translation…at least not as we understand the word "eternity."

While Mr. Morgan was a life-long student of the Bible, we should not take his opinion on this matter without further study. The most important thing we learn from him is that not all qualified Bible teachers are in agreement on the issue of "eternity." When I first took my stand as to the beliefs expressed in this book, I was quickly challenged and told that the Greek word "aionian" which is found throughout the New Testament means, and has always meant, "eternal." As we can see, not all studied men and women agree on this point. Many will stand up today and tell you that "aionian" **must be** translated "eternal." Mr. Morgan is just one example of a well studied man who would disagree.

WHAT CAN WE LEARN FROM THE BIBLE ITSELF?

You can buy a Greek study book, and depending on the author you may find that "aionian" means "eternal," or you may find that it means "age-abiding." You can read the translation of the Bible you have chosen, placing your faith in the translators…that they got it right. You can listen to your pastor or your professor. You can read the opinions of men like G. Campbell Morgan or others who have written on the topic.

Or…you can look at the Bible and see for yourself!

You don't need to be a Greek scholar. Read on!

INCONSISTENCIES IN THE TRANSLATIONS

In most cases our common English translators have taken the Greek word "aionian" or "aion" and translated it "eternal", "eternity", "forever", or some such word as these meaning endless. In many of these cases the word is referring to God Himself, or to "eternal life" or "eternal damnation."

19

But the translators encounter many difficulties, because in a fair number of cases the **same word** is used ("aionian" or "aion") and it cannot possibly mean endless.

To give you a quick summary, the words "aion" and "aionian" occur 199 times in the New Testament. In the King James Version the word is translated "ages" 2 times, "course" one time, "world" 43 times, and "eternal" or some variation the remaining 153 times. So in 46 of of the 199 times where we find the word "aion" or "aionian" (or 23% of the time) the King James Version recognizes that the word cannot be properly translated "eternal," since it is clearly a limited duration being expressed.

How could God, who is wanting to reveal things to us through the Bible, confuse us by using a single word that sometimes means "eternity" while other times carries a very different meaning? I realize that when we translate from the Greek it is sometimes necessary to use English "idiom" or expression to relay the meaning...but could a single Greek word carry such opposite meanings as "eternal" and "temporary?"

LET'S LOOK AT JUST A FEW SAMPLE PASSAGES OF SCRIPTURE

Compare the following passages. Note that in the Concordant Literal New Testament (CLNT) translation when the word "aionian" or "aion" is found, the English equivalent "eonian" or "eon" is used.

Ephesians 2:7

> "That in the *__ages__* to come he might shew the exceeding riches of his grace..." (KJV)
> "that in the coming *__ages__* he might show the incomparable riches of his grace..." (NIV)
> "that, in the oncoming *__eons__*, He should be displaying the transcendent riches..." (CLNT)

Colossians 1:26

"the mystery which hath been hid from ***ages*** and from generations, but now is made manifest to his saints:" (KJV)

"the mystery that has been kept hidden for ***ages*** and generations, but is now disclosed to the saints." (NIV)

"the secret which has been concealed from the ***eons*** and from the generations, yet now was made manifest to His saints..." (CLNT)

Matthew 12:32

"And whosoever speaketh a word against the Son of man, it shall be forgiven him; but whosoever speaketh against the Holy Ghost, it shall not be forgiven him, neither in this ***world***, neither in the world to come." (KJV)

"Anyone who speaks a word against the Son of Man will be forgiven, but anyone who speaks against the Holy Spirit will not be forgiven, either in this ***age*** or in the age to come." (NIV)

"And whosoever may be saying a word against the Son of Mankind, it will be pardoned him, yet whoever may be saying aught against the holy spirit, it shall not be pardoned him, neither in this ***eon*** nor in that which is impending." (CLNT)

Matthew 13:22

"...the care of this ***world***, and the deceitfulness of riches, choke the word..." (KJV)

"...the worries of this ***life*** and the deceitfulness of wealth choke it..." (NIV)

"...the worry of this ***eon*** and the seduction of riches are stifling the word..." (CLNT)

1 Timothy 6:17

"Charge them that are rich in this ***world***..." (KJV)

"Command those who are rich in this present ***world***..." (NIV)

"Those who are rich in the current ***eon***..." (CLNT)

In these cases the NIV and KJV translators recognize from the context that "aion" cannot mean "eternal." Yet much of the time the translators have used the word "eternal" (or some variation) to translate the **same** Greek word:

2 Corinthians 9:9
> "...his righteousness remaineth for **_ever_**" (KJV)
> "...his righteousness endures **_forever_**." (NIV)
> "...His righteousness remains for the **_eon_**." (CLNT)

John 11:26
> "And whosoever liveth and believeth in me shall **_never_** die." (KJV)
> "...and whoever lives and believes in me will **_never_** die." (NIV)
> "And everyone who is living and believing in Me, should by no means be dying for the **_eon_**." (CLNT)

John 14:16
> "...he shall give you another Comforter, that he may abide with you for **_ever_**/" (KJV)
> "...and he will give you another Counselor to be with you **_forever_**..." (NIV)
> "...and He will be giving you another consoler, that it, indeed, may be with you for the **_eon_**..." (CLNT)

Galations 1:4-5
> "...that he might deliver us from this present evil **_world_**, according to the will of God and our Father: To whom be glory for **_ever and ever_**." (KJV)
> "...to rescue us from the present evil **_age_**, according to the will of our God and Father, to whom be glory for **_ever and ever_**." (NIV)

"...that He might extricate us out of the present wicked ***eon***, according to the will of our God and Father, to Whom be glory for the ***eons of the eons.***" (CLNT)

NOTE: This passage is very interesting, since the same Greek word (aion) is used twice in two verses, and is translated "forever" in one instance and "world"(or "age") in the other (since it could not possibly mean "forever"). While the word "world" may seem to fit "aion" in some cases, it clearly does not fit in others. Therefore the thought that God was trying to convey when using the word "aion" cannot be "world." Furthermore, God uses another totally different word to relay the concept "world" – the Greek "kosmos."

Revelation 11:15

"The kingdoms of this world are become the kingdoms of our Lord, and of his Christ; and he shall reign for ***ever and ever.***" (KJV)

"The kingdom of the world has become the kingdom of our Lord and of his Christ, and he will reign for ***ever and ever***." (NIV)

"The kingdom of this world became our Lord's and his Christ's, and He shall be reigning for the ***eons of the eons!***" (CLNT)

*NOTE: Here is another interesting passage. Take the NIV for instance, where we read that Christ will reign for ever and ever. But look at 1 Corinthians 15:25 in the same NIV translation, where we read that "he must reign **until** he has put all his enemies under his feet." A few verses later in 1 Corinthians 15:28 we read, "When he has done this, then the Son himself will be made subject to him who put everything under him, so that God may be All in all." This is obviously a contradiction, for if Christ reigns **for ever and ever** how can he reign "**until**" the time that he stops reigning and turns the kingdom over to God?*

Revelation 20:10

> "and shall be tormented day and night for ***ever and ever.***" (KJV)
> "They will be tormented day and night for ***ever and ever.***" (NIV)
> "And they shall be tormented day and night for the ***eons of the eons***." (CLNT)

It is clear what has happened. The translators saw the passages referring to God, and Christ's reign, and the torment of the wicked, and the "eternal" life of the saved, and figured that aion and aionian had to mean "forever." They reasoned that God is eternal and life for the Believer must be eternal, so therefore "aion" must mean eternal, at least in these scripture references. And if life for the Believer is eternal, so also punishment for the unsaved must be eternal since the same "aionian" is found in these references.

But even when "aion" or "aionian" are properly translated, God's Word does not limit what will happen ***after*** the end of the ages. The translators chose to ***change the meaning of certain words found in Scripture*** to give you their opinions. Where they felt "aion" had to mean eternal…it was translated as such. Where they knew it could not mean eternal…another word was chosen.

This is not intended to be a comprehensive analysis of every occurrence of "aion" or "aionian." Refer to the books listed in the final chapter if you are interested in studying more along these lines.

But from these few passages we can see:

1. There is inconsistency in how the word "aion" or "aionian" is translated, and
2. There are at least some cases within the Bible where the word cannot possibly mean "eternity," as is even acknowledged by our common English translations, since they were forced to use a different word in these cases.

Let's consider a few other things!

HOW MANY ETERNITIES ARE THERE?

If "aion" is eternity, what would "aions" mean? If "aion" is endless, how can there be more than that? But in some passages, "aion" is singular while in other passages we find the plural "aions."

    Ephesians 2:7   "the oncoming eons"
    Colossians 1:26   "concealed from the eons"

WHAT DOES "BEFORE ETERNITY" MEAN?

If "aion" is eternity, what is meant by *__before__* eternity?

    2 Timothy 1:9   "before times eonian"
    Titus 1:2   "before times eonian"
    1 Corinthians 2:7 "before the eons"

WHAT DOES THE "END OF ETERNITY" MEAN?

If "aion" is eternity, what is meant by "the end of the aions?" Could there be an end to eternity, or something "after eternity?" This phrase alone should be enough to show us that "aion" cannot mean "forever."

    Matthew 13:39   "the conclusion of the eon"
    Matthew 24:3   "the conclusion of the eon"
    1 Corinthians 10:11 "the consummations of the eons"
    Hebrews 9:26   "at the conclusion of the eons"

Actually, look at 1 Corinthians 15, because that talks about what happens at "the consummation" at the end of the ages. All enemies are defeated. The final enemy (death) is abolished. Christ, who has been reigning as the eons come to an end, subjects Himself to the Father, and God becomes All in all.

SOME VERY SPECIFIC "EONS" ARE NOTED IN SCRIPTURE

In Galations 1:4 we read of "the present wicked eon." What would "the present wicked eternity" mean?

In Ephesians 2:7 we read of "the oncoming eons." If we live in the middle of eternity, what would "the eternity to come" mean?

2 Corinthians 4:4 speaks of the Adversary as "the god of this eon." Would the Adversary (Satan) be referred to as "the god of eternity?"

CONSIDER THE MANY DIFFERENT VARIATIONS OF "EON"

Look very closely at each word...

Hebrews 1:8	"the eon of the eon"
Ephesians 3:21	"the eon of the eons"
Galations 1:5	"the eons of the eons"

If "eon" is eternity, what do these things mean?

If "eon," however, does not mean eternity, it makes all the sense in the world. If there are a number of eons, or ages, referred to in the Bible, these various expressions can really tell us something.

"The eon of the eon" would refer to a single eon of time, as it relates to the previous eon (in other words, the eon that resulted from or that came out of the previous eon).

"The eon of the eons" would refer to a single eon (or age) out of a group of two or more eons.

"The eons of the eons" would refer to two or more eons in relation to the other eons. For example, there are times within Scripture when

26

the final two eons are referred to as compared with all of the other eons. Christ will reign for these two eons:

> The first beginning when Christ returns to the earth and sends Satan to the "submerged chaos" (the "Abyss" in the NIV) and begins His reign upon the earth – Revelation 20:1-3
>
> The second beginning when the current heaven and earth pass away (see Matthew 24:35) and the new heaven and new earth appear – Revelation 21.

Incidentally, the structure of these phrases, speaking of an "eon" as it relates to the other "eons," is the same word structure used in the Bible for:

Hebrews 9:1 "the holy place" (same word structure as "the eon")

Hebrews 9:3 "the holy of holies" (same word structure as "the eon of the eons")

Hebrews 9:25 "the holies of holies" (same word structure as "the eons of the eons")

In each case, a specific place within the tabernacle is described as it relates to the other portions of the tabernacle. Likewise in the "eonian" examples, a single eon (or several eons) is described as it relates to the other eons.

The idea of "forever" has come from tradition and the theology of mankind. Throughout God's Word He speaks of limited (albeit long) periods of time called "eons."

If you think about it from our school days we remember the word "eon" being used to describe a very long time. We will sometimes even use the expression, "it has been eons" to mean that it has been a very long time.

I once had a well-meaning friend tell me that I should consult with the seminary professors who were Greek experts, and who would

27

inform me that "aionian" always means "eternal." I say to you that it doesn't take a scholar or a Greek expert to see from Scripture itself that "aion" and "aionian" cannot possibly mean "eternal."

Furthermore, because our translators and the churches of our day insist upon arguing for an "eternal" meaning for "aion," much of the truth in God's Word is now very hard to see unless you are willing to do some study beyond your modern English Bible translation.

GOD'S PURPOSE OF THE EONS

When talking about the "eons" (or "ages") as described in God's Word, some who would defend the translation "eternity" will tell you that to cut up the Bible into ages (some would call them dispensations) is to destroy the unity of the Bible. But if God has purposed to work out His plan through the ages, acting in different ways in different ages as He works toward the goal of becoming "All in all" (1 Corinthians 15), what right do we have to ignore the specific eons that God has told us about in His Word, by translating the word so erratically.

Ephesians 3:11   "in accord with the *purpose* of the eons"

We get a glimpse of this grand purpose in the following passages:

Ephesians 1:8-11 "to head up all in the Christ – both that in the heavens and that on the earth…operating all in accord with the counsel of His will…"

Philippians 2:9-11 "that in the name of Jesus every knee should be bowing, celestial and terrestrial and subterranean, and every tongue should be acclaiming that Jesus Christ is Lord, for the glory of God, the Father."

28

Colossians 1:15-21   "…and through Him (Christ) to reconcile all to Him…"

1 Corinthians 15:20ff The consummation…with God becoming All in all.

The Bible tells us about the time period known as "the eons" (or ages) when God works toward the ultimate fulfillment of His purposes.

A FEW OTHER NOTABLE OPINIONS CONCERNING "AIONIAN"

Marvin Vincent, author of "Word Studies in the New Testament" says of "aionian" (see his notes on 2 Thessalonians 1:9),

> "(It is) a period of time of longer or shorter duration, having a beginning and an end, and complete in itself…The word always carries the notion of ***time***, and not of ***eternity***. It always means a period of time. Otherwise it would be impossible to account for the plural, or for such qualifying expressions as ***this*** age, or the age ***to come***. It does not mean something endless or everlasting…The adjective…in like manner carries the idea of time. Neither the noun nor the adjective, in themselves, carry the sense of endless or everlasting…Words which are ***habitually*** applied to things temporal or material cannot carry in themselves the sense of endlessness.
> Even when applied to God, we are not forced to render (the word) everlasting. Of course the life of God is endless; but the question is whether, in describing God (by this Greek word), it was intended to describe the duration of His being, or whether some different and larger idea was not contemplated."

As we have seen in our brief look at a few selected passages of Scripture, these are some very astute observations relative to the words "aion" and "aionian."

29

Dr. F. W. Farrar said, "...aion, aionios and their Hebrew equivalents in all combinations are repeatedly used of things which have come to an end."

Even Augustine admits that in Scripture "aion" and "aionios" must in many cases mean "having an end."

"The Concise Dictionary of English Etymology," first published in 1882 by Walter Skeat, reports that our English word "eternal" comes from the Latin "aternus" which means, literally, "lasting for an age." Professor Max Muller agrees, saying that "aeternum" originally signified life or time, but has given rise to a number of words expressing eternity – the very opposite of life and time.

Webster's New World Dictionary provides the following definition for "eon."

> "an age, lifetime, eternity...an extremely long, indefinite period of time; thousands and thousands of years."

From "Salvator Mundi, or Is Christ the Saviour of All Men?" by Samuel Cox:

> "No doubt it was right at one time to translate *aeonial* by *eternal*, and would be right again could we reinstate the original significance of the word: for, strangely enough, the word 'eternal' originally meant aeonial or age-long. It comes to us from the Latin *aeternus*, the older and longer form of which is *aeviternus*: and the word *aevum*, which is the root of it, is simply the Latin form of the Greek *aion* and the English *aeon*." (page 119)

Cox notes in this work a quotation from Charles Kingsley:

> "The word aion is never used in Scripture or anywhere else in the sense of endlessness (vulgarly called eternity). It always meant, both in Scripture and out, a period of time. Else how could it have a plural—And how could you talk of the aeons,

and aeons of aeons, as the Scripture does? Nay, more, how talk of 'outos o aion' (this age), which the translators, with laudable inconsistency, have translated 'this world', i.e., the present state of things, age, dispensation, or epoch. Aionios therefore means, and must mean, belonging to an epoch, or the epoch; and "aionios kolasis" (aeonial punishment) is the punishment allotted to that epoch." (page 122)

William Barclay, well known Greek expert and author of the popular "Daily Study Bible Series" says in his autobiography:

"The word for eternal is aionios. It means more than everlasting, for Plato (who may have invented the word) plainly says that a thing may be everlasting and still not be aionios. The simplest way to put it is that aionios cannot be used properly of anyone but God; it is the word uniquely, as Plato saw it, of God. Eternal punishment is then literally that kind of remedial punishment which it befits God to give and which only God can give."

WHY WOULD GOD HAVE ALLOWED ERROR TO CREEP IN?

I once had a man argue that God would not have allowed our translations to become filled with error. He determined from this that "aion" had to mean "eternal" because most modern translations use this word, and God would not have allowed us to be misled.

First, there are reliable translations and other Bible study materials that will allow you to study the Scriptures if you are willing to dig deeper. If you are willing to look beyond the common translations, you can find the truth.

Second, if you use a modern English translation you will still see the way to salvation (through Jesus Christ, the Son of God) and you will still see many of the principles and truths pertaining to God. But the deeper truths God has revealed will be hidden!

31

TRUST IN GOD'S WORD; NOT IN THE TRANSLATION

I have faith that the Bible is indeed the very Word of God. I have considered the evidence and have settled this matter through my personal study. But I do not have faith in the modern English translations when it comes to a detailed study of God's Word. If I want to study to learn the deeper truths of God's revelation, I will use some of the books and reference materials noted in the final chapter, and would highly recommend them to you.

THINK FOR YOURSELF!

Once, as I explained my views pertaining to God's "eonian" purpose, a minister replied, "I often thought there might be something after eternity." He could sense that some things just didn't add up when it came to reading his modern English translation, and considering the love and the will of God.

If eternity is really eternity (as we would define the word today) it would be impossible for there to be anything which came after. The fact of the matter is that the modern English translators have mistranslated the words "aion" and "aionian." They got it wrong, and there is now a great deal of "orthodox pressure" to keep things the way they are.

As we have seen, "aion" and "aionian" do not mean "eternity." As you read your Bible, keep this in mind!

FOR FURTHER STUDY

I have tried to keep this short study basic, recognizing that you can study from other sources if you are interested in learning more. I did want to be complete enough to show you why, beyond a shadow of doubt, I have been convinced that "aion" and "aionian" do not mean eternal, and this has some very major implications that we will explore in upcoming chapters.

If you would like to do more study on the various occurrences of "aion" and "aionian" in Scripture, I would refer you to the books listed in the final chapter, especially those noted that include specific teachings on the matter of "aionian."

Chapter Four

HOW MANY AGES ARE THERE?

If there are different eons (or ages) referred to in Scripture, how many eons (or ages) are there? A detailed study would be a book in itself, and some of the information provided in Scripture is vague and has been interpreted in different ways. Some say there are five eons; others six.

As I do not wish to make this work speculative, I will lay out only those facts concerning the eons that are indisputable. I will not take a stand as to how many eons God has established, but will instead simply show you the individual eons that God clearly makes reference to.

BEFORE THE EONS
The Bible refers to a time "before the eons" began.

2 Timothy 1:9-10	"grace which is given to us in Christ Jesus *before times eonian*."
Titus 1:1-3	God's promises were made *"before times eonian*."
1 Corinthians 2:6-8	God's wisdom designated *"before the eons*."

THE CURRENT EON
Much more information is revealed concerning the current eon...the age in which we live.

34

Matthew 12:32	*"this eon"*
Matthew 13:22	"the worry of *this eon*"
Mark 4:19	"the worries of *this eon*"
Luke 16:8	"the sons of *this eon*"
Luke 20:34	"The sons of *this eon*"
Romans 12:2	"not to be configured to *this eon*"
1 Corinthians 1:20	*"this eon"*
1 Corinthians 2:6-8	"a wisdom not of *this eon*"
1 Corinthians 3:18	"If anyone among you is presuming to be wise in *this eon*"
2 Corinthians 4:4	"the god of *this eon*"
Galations 1:3-5	*"the present wicked eon"*
1 Timothy 6:17	"Those who are rich in *the current eon*"
2 Timothy 4:9-10	"Demas, loving *the current eon*, forsook me"
Titus 2:11-13	"we should be living sanely and justly and devoutly in *the current eon*"

Two passages which make reference to the current eon are worthy of special attention.

Ephesians 2:2   "in accord with *the eon of this world*"

In some cases our modern English translations have used the word "world" for eon, but here we see that a clearly different idea is intended, since both "aion" and "kosmos" are used in the same sentence ("eon" and "world"). The KJV translates this passage "according to the *course* of this *world*."

Ephesians 1:21   "not only in *this eon*, but also in that which is impending"

This single passage makes reference to two different eons, making it very clear that there is *"this eon"* (in which we live) and there will be a forthcoming eon; *"that which is impending."*

35

THE IMPENDING EON

When this current eon has concluded there will be another eon forthcoming.

Matthew 12:32	"neither in this eon nor in that which is *impending*"
Mark 10:30	Those following Jesus to receive, "in the *coming eon*, life eonian"
Luke 18:30	Those following Jesus to receive, "in the *coming eon*, life eonian"
Luke 20:35	"*that eon*" is compared with "this eon"
Ephesians 1:21	"not only in this eon, but also in *that which is impending*"
Hebrews 6:5	"of the *impending eon*"

AT LEAST TWO EONS TO COME

Jude 1:25 uses the phrase "*for all the eons.*" We have looked at passages that referenced a time before the eons began, but as to the "eons" we read about in Scripture, how many are there? Thus far we have read about:

1. This current eon
2. An eon to come

But Ephesians 2:7 speaks of "*the oncoming eons*" (plural), indicating that in the future there will be at least two eons to come. Therefore we see thus far in God's Word three separate eons:

1. This current eon
2. An eon to come
3. Another eon to come after that

As to these "oncoming eons," they are referred to in a number of ways.

THE EON OF THE EONS

Ephesians 3:21 uses the phrase "the eon of the eons," which seems to make reference to a single eon as compared with the other eons.

Hebrews 1:8 uses a similar phrase, "the eon of the eon," which seems to make reference to a single eon which proceeds out of (or follows) the previous eon.

THE EONS OF THE EONS

This frequently used phrase makes reference to at least two eons as compared with all of the other eons. It appears to make reference to the last two eons:

- One eon which begins when Christ returns to reign upon the earth for 1000 years (the "millennial kingdom").

- The eon which follows, when the new heavens and earth are created, and with Christ still reigning.

You can study the various occurrences of the phrase "eons of the eons" in the following passages:

Romans 16:27; Galations 1:5; Philippians 4:20; 1 Timothy 1:17; 2 Timothy 4:18; Hebrews 13:21; 1 Peter 4:11; 1 Peter 5:11; Revelation 1:6,18; Revelation 4:9,10; Revelation 5:13; Revelation 7:12; Revelation 10:6; Revelation 11:15; Revelation 14:11; Revelation 15:7; Revelation 19:3; Revelation 20:10; Revelation 22:5

"FOR THE EON" AND "EONIAN"

An "eon" is a distinct period of time. When the expression "for the eon" is used, it refers to something that is happening during a specific eon. Likewise the expression "for the eons" or "for all the eons" refers to something that is happening during multiple eons, or even during all of the eons.

"Eonian" is the adjective form of "eon," and is used in a variety of ways in Scripture:

Eonian times
Eonian life
Eonian salvation
Eonian redemption
Eonian covenant
Eonian allotment
Eonian kingdom
Eonian evangel
Eonian consolation
Eonian glory
Eonian God
Eonian fire/punishment

These phrases speak of things that may last for a single eon, for multiple eons, or for all of the eons. Each passage must be studied to determine which is the case. (Note: The Keyword Concordance which is included in the CLNT will enable the reader to study each reference containing the word "eon" or "eonian.")

But once the eons have ended this does not mean that these things that are "eonian" must end. The phrase "eonian God," for example, speaks of God as He works in the eons. When the eons conclude, this does not mean that God ceases to exist, as we see in 1 Corinthians 15 when God becomes "All in all" after the eons have ended.

In other cases, though, things that exist in the eons may end when the eons have concluded. The "eonian kingdom," for example, ends at the consummation of the eons (1 Corinthians 15) when Christ delivers up the kingdom to God, and when there is no longer a need for "sovereignty, authority, or power." God concludes the ages by becoming All in all.

Likewise, at the consummation when the final enemy (death) is abolished and when God becomes All in all, fulfilling His ultimate purpose, there will no longer be a need for the fire and punishment that had existed during the eons, for they will have fulfilled their purpose.

THE CONCLUSION (END) OF THE EON

Jesus uses the phrase "conclusion of the eon" several times. Note that "eon" is singular, and Jesus is referring to the end of a particular eon, before the next eon begins.

Matthew 13:39	"the harvest is the *conclusion of the eon.*"
Matthew 13:49	"Thus shall it be in the *conclusion of the eon.*"
Matthew 24:3	"what is the sign of Thy presence and of the *conclusion of the eon.*"
Matthew 28:20	"till the *conclusion of the eon.*"

So again we see that an eon is a period of time that has an ending.

THE CONCLUSION (END) OF THE EONS

Another phrase is used in Scripture; "the conclusion of the eons" (plural) which refers to the end of all eons, or ages.

Hebrews 9:26 speaks of Christ's sacrifice, and notes that "at the conclusion of the eons" He is manifest for the repudiation of sin through His sacrifice. While His sacrifice has taken place long ago, and while many in this present age have been reconciled through His work upon the cross, at the end of the eons He will be manifest that the fullness of His work will be accomplished.

The ultimate passage which speaks of the end of the eons is 1 Corinthians 15:20-28.

"Yet now Christ has been roused from among the dead,
the Firstfruit of those who are reposing.

"For since, in fact, through a man came death,

through a Man, also, comes the resurrection of the dead.

"For even as, in Adam, all are dying,
thus also, in Christ, shall all be vivified.

"Yet each in his own class:
the Firstfruit, Christ;
thereupon those who are Christ's in His presence;
thereafter **the consummation**,

"whenever He may be giving up the kingdom to His God and Father,

"whenever He should be nullifying all sovereignty and all authority and power.
For He must be reigning until He should be placing all His enemies under His feet.

"The last enemy is being abolished: death.

"For He subjects all under His feet...

"then the Son Himself also shall be subjected to Him...
that God may be All in all."

THE PURPOSE OF THE EONS

Ephesians 1:11 points out that God "is operating all in accord with the counsel of His will." Similarly in Ephesians 3:9-11 we find that the eons have a purpose. Here Paul writes that he has been granted grace,

"to bring the evangel
of the untraceable riches of Christ to the nations,

"and to enlighten all
as to what is the administration of the secret,

"which has been concealed from the eons in God,
Who creates all,

"that now may be made known
to the sovereignties and the authorities among the celestials, through the ecclesia,

"the multifarious wisdom of God,
in accord with the purpose of the eons
which He makes in Christ Jesus, our Lord…"

Since there was a time before the eons existed, and a time after the eons end, why did God bring into existence this period of time referred to as "the eons?" We see here that the eons have a purpose. And since God is operating all in accord with the counsel of His will, we understand that He is using "the eons" to accomplish His purposes; ultimately leading all things toward "the consummation" at the end of the eons, when God becomes All in all. (1 Corinthians 15:28)

Romans 11:36 tells us that all is "out of God." 1 Corinthians 15:28 tells us that God will ultimately be "All in all." The eons are the period of time between, which God uses to accomplish His will and His purposes.

WHAT IS THE POINT?

While I have not attempted to show how many specific eons are mentioned in Scripture, I have desired to show that **there are distinct, separate eons (or ages) that are mentioned in God's Word.** These "eons" are periods of time with a beginning and an end.

There was a time before these eons began. There will be a time when all of the eons will come to an end. We have seen at least three distinct eons referred to in God's Word.

These distinctions are lost in most modern English translations since there is no consistency in translation, and it is impossible to see the various eons that God speaks of. Our goal in this chapter has been to reveal these distinctions, so that we can see God systematically working to accomplish His purposes and His will through the eons, or ages.

Chapter Five

WHAT ABOUT HELL & JUDGMENT?

Another word that is grossly misunderstood is "hell." I had always been taught that those who believe in Jesus Christ as Saviour *in this lifetime* will spend eternity in heaven, and those who do not believe in Jesus Christ as Saviour *in this lifetime* will spend eternity in hell, tormented forever by the flames as the just punishment for their disbelief.

These things, I was taught, are what the Bible say. Is this true?

HELL
In our English translations, three different Greek words are thrown together and translated with the single word "hell."

"Hades": Used 11 times in the New Testament
Translated "hell" 10 times and "grave" once in KJV

"Gehenna": Used 12 times in the New Testament
Translated "hell" all 12 times in KJV

"Tartarus": Used only once in the New Testament
Translated "hell" in KJV

In the Old Testament we find the Hebrew,

"Sheol": Used 65 times in the Old Testament
Translated "hell" 31 times, "grave" 31 times and "pit" 3 times in KJV

As was the case with "aionian" we see some of the same inconsistent treatment of the Hebrew word "sheol." As we have come to think of "hell" today, there is a big difference between "hell" and "grave," although both are used as translations for the same Hebrew word. If you were to use a concordance to look at every passage where "sheol" is used, you will see why the translators used "grave" in many instances. It is because "hell" as we understand it would not be an appropriate translation.

Psalm 16:10 "For thou wilt not leave my soul in hell" (KJV)

THIS IS DAVID SPEAKING! Would David be in hell? Here is an example of an incorrect translation of "sheol," which should be rendered "unseen place." (The NIV translates sheol "grave" in this instance.)

HADES IS THE EQUIVALENT OF SHEOL

Acts 2:27,31 makes a direct reference to the Psalm 16 passage we just looked at. Here we see that "hades" is the Greek equivalent for the Hebrew "sheol."

"For Thou wilt not be forsaking my soul in the *unseen*" (v 27)

"He was neither forsaken in the *unseen* nor was His flesh acquainted with decay." (v 31)

Note that the Concordant Literal translation for "hades" is "unseen."

With this inspired passage, we find that "hades" in the New Testament (Greek) should be interpreted in the same way as "sheol" in the Old Testament (Hebrew).

WHAT IS THE PENALTY FOR SIN?

In Genesis 2:17 God decreed the penalty for sin:

> "From every tree of the garden, you are to eat, yea, eat. Yet from the tree of the knowledge of good and evil, you are not to be eating from it, for in the day you eat from it, to die shall you be dying." (CVOT)

In Chapter 3 of Genesis we see the sin of Adam and Eve, and the penalty for sin is executed. They were expelled from the garden, expelled from the presence of God, and prohibited to eat any longer from the tree of life. The process of dying has begun, in accordance with the penalty for sin, "Dying, thou dost die."

Is the penalty for sin death, or is it an eternity of tormenting in hell?

To be our Saviour, Jesus Christ suffered the penalty for sin on our behalf. Did he suffer death, or did he suffer an eternity in hell in order to pay our debt? The resurrection is proof that *every claim of righteousness* was fulfilled by Christ.

WHERE DID THE NOTION OF "HELL" COME FROM?

Our present day notion of "hell" as a place where the wicked and unsaved will be tormented in fire for eternity comes not from the Word of God, but from pagan philosophy and myth. The Greeks saw Hades as the spirit world, or an intermediate state. Their myths developed images of Hades that have been preserved to the present day.

The well known "Dante's Inferno," by Dante Alighiere (1265-1321 A.D.) comes from "Divine Comedy," the story of a fictitious trip through heaven, hell and purgatory. Dante was a great poet, and he exerted a strong influence on society in his day.

We have allowed these pagan ideas of "hell" to taint our understanding of the Word of God. Dante, and those creating the myths of old, misused the Greek "hades." Whereas "hades" simply refers to "the unseen place," the myths painted a fictitious picture as to this place. They have described in detail this place that no living person has ever seen, and much of our thinking about death, what happens to us after death, and the "after-life" has come from these writers, not from the Word of God.

As used in the Word of God, "sheol" and "hades" are not describing the same thing as Dante or the myth writers of old, as we can clearly see when examining every occurrence of these words in the Bible.

Many great preachers have proclaimed a message of a fiery, eternal hell. Jonathan Edwards and C. H. Spurgeon are two of the greatest preachers in history, but their eloquence does not make them right. Certainly they preached the truth in many areas, but when it comes to the subject of hell they were clearly basing their beliefs on the incorrect English translations and the incorrect "orthodox" doctrines available to them. Unbeknownst to them, they preached of a hell based upon the pagan images they had inherited, and not upon the truth of God's Word.

Let us look to God's Word to understand the destiny of mankind, and not to images created by pagan writers which taint God's character.

DEATH

A close study of Scripture will show us that individuals do not go immediately to heaven (or to hell) immediately upon death. Some will use a few isolated passages of Scripture—misinterpreted, used out of context, or mistranslated—to justify the position that the saved go immediately to heaven. This is a study unto itself, and well worth your serious exploration into God's Word.

For now, though, let us look at how "death" is described in the Scriptures.

Ecclesiastes 12:7 (CVOT)

> "And the soil (referring to the physical body) returns to the earth just as it was, And the spirit, it returns to the One, Elohim (God), Who gave it."

Consider the example of Jesus. At the point of death He committed His spirit to the Father (Luke 23:46), His soul was in "hades" (Acts 2:27,31), and His body was buried in the grave (soil). The only difference in Jesus' case was that God preserved His body from decay (Acts 2:31).

In short, death is a return to the original state of existence before God brought the elements (soil and spirit) together to form a living soul. The body, created from the elements of the earth (soil) return to the earth (soil). The spirit which was "breathed into" the body to form life returns to God. The soul, which did not exist before God created life, returns to the "unseen."

The soul, in "hades" or the "unseen" place, has no consciousness. Consider the following passages.

> "For the living know that they shall die: but the dead know not any thing." Ecclesiastes 9:5 (KJV)

> "No one remembers you when he is dead." Psalm 6:5 (NIV)

As we can see, even our common KJV and NIV translations tell us that the dead are not in a conscious state. In some cases death is even equated to sleep (a state of unconsciousness):

Psalm 13:3   "I will sleep in death." (NIV)

Daniel 12:2   "Multitudes who sleep in the dust of the earth will awake." (NIV)

1 Thessalonians 4:13 "But I would not have you to be ignorant, brethren, concerning them which are asleep." (KJV)

Death, then, is simply a dissolution or dis-assembly of the body and the spirit, and the soul that was created at the union of the body and the spirit. The soul sleeps in the "unseen" place, awaiting the resurrection. As we consider those of our friends who have died, truly they have gone to an "unseen" place. One day they lived in our midst, and the next we no longer see them, or hear them, or touch them.

Some may protest, "Are you saying my loved ones are not in heaven at this moment?" I, too, had been taught for years that upon death one goes immediately to heaven or to hell for eternity, but this is not supported by Scripture.

As I write these words I mourn the very recent loss of a dear cousin, barely 50 years old, who will be committed to the grave in the next few days. Knowing he is asleep at this moment instead of in heaven causes me no concern. Either way I will be mourning his loss in this lifetime, and I grieve with his family at the loss they have endured. But I do not mourn as those who have no hope. I praise God and marvel at His grace and His love, knowing that Chuck is now asleep, awaiting the miraculous day of resurrection which is foretold and assured in the Word of God!

INCONSISTENCIES IN THE ENGLISH TRANSLATIONS

Some English translators determine that the evil must go to hell, and they translate sheol as "hell" in Psalm 9:17

"The wicked shall be turned into **_hell_**, and all the nations that forget God" (KJV)

Others are more accurate, translating sheol as "grave" in this passage instead of "hell."

"The wicked return to the **_grave_**, all the nations that forget God." (NIV)

Consider Job 30:23, where both the KJV and NIV translate sheol as "death."

"I know you will bring me down to **_death_**, to the place appointed for all the living." (NIV)

"For I know that thou wilt bring me to **_death_**, and to the house appointed for all the living." (KJV)

Is this not a major inconsistency in the KJV? Job 30:23 says that **_death_** is the lot for "all the living." But the very same word, "sheol," is translated **_hell_** in Psalm 9:17. In the Psalm 9 passage the bias of the translators has crept in. They determined in their reasoning that the wicked must be going to **_hell_**. But they could not treat the word "sheol" in a consistent manner in the Job passage, since we are told that "sheol" is the place where "all the living" will go.

A CLOSER LOOK AT "SHEOL" AND "HADES"

"Hades" is a word constructed from the following Greek roots:

"a"   un
"idein"   to perceive

The "h" at the beginning of "hades" comes from a breathing mark which affects the pronunciation of the otherwise "ades."

The word construction would infer a meaning of "unseen" for the Greek "hades."

"Sheol" in all cases is concerned with the state of death, where all human activities cease. It, too, could be properly translated "unseen." We have seen in the case of "sheol" that the word could not possibly mean the popular notion of "hell," since "sheol" is a place where not only the wicked go, but where **_all_** will go.

Both "sheol" and the Greek equivalent "hades" would indicate that "unseen place" where all who die go, saved or unsaved, to await the resurrection.

GEHENNA

"Gehenna" is a word not used by any Greek authors. It appears to be the Greek spelling for the Hebrew "Gai Hinnom," or "Valley of Hinnom." The "Valley of Hinnom," or "Gehenna," is not a spiritual place like our notion of "hell." It is an actual, physical place.

In 2 Chronicles 28:3 and 33:6 it is a place where the Jews would sacrifice and burn their children in idolatry. King Josiah, when making his reforms, "defiled" the place "so as to lure no one to make his son or his daughter pass through fire to Molech." (2 Kings 23:10)

Later the place was used as a garbage dump. In Jesus' day, fires burned in Gehenna to destroy the refuse of Jerusalem.

Much of our problem is that when we hear Jesus talk about the kingdom in the gospels, we think He is talking about heaven. This is what I was always taught. The kingdom and heaven have been confused, just as the translations of "aionian" and "hades/sheol" have been confused.

The Old Testament prophets talked about a return of the physical kingdom, like the one in David's day, except with the Lord Himself upon the throne. This is often referred to as the "millennial kingdom" or the 1000 year reign. This future millennial kingdom will be a physical kingdom upon the earth. As you read through the New Testament, pay close attention to every detail, and you will see that the description of the kingdom shows us it is a very physical place. The "Sermon on the Mount" is the code of laws that will be enforced when the kingdom is set up.

When Jesus mentions "Gehenna" for the first time (in Matthew), as He is introducing the coming Kingdom upon the earth, his hearers knew He was referring to the Valley of Hinnom, and that casting one into this refuse dump for Kingdom violations was the topic. Had Jesus been introducing, for the first time ever, the concept of an eternal torment, there would have been questions, as this would have been an entirely new concept. Up until now the penalty for sin has been death, and not an eternal torment. This has been the case since death was introduced as the penalty early in Genesis, and it has been the case throughout the entire Old Testament. Now, as Jesus talks about Gehenna, if He is introducing a new punishment, questions would have been raised and a further explanation given.

A complete study of "The Kingdom" would be a book unto itself. I simply ask you to consider what I have just said as you re-study and re-think your way through the New Testament once again.

So "Gehenna," or the "Valley of Hinnom," was a physical refuse dump since Old Testament times, and in the days of Jesus. From Jesus' words we see that it will again play a role in the upcoming millenial kingdom, where immediate judgment will be meted out for transgressions, and where those committing crimes worthy of death will be cast into the "Valley of Hinnom."

> "Yet whoever may be saying to his brother, 'Raka!' shall be liable to the Sanhedrin. Yet whoever may be saying, 'Stupid!' shall be liable to the Gehenna of fire." (Matthew 5:22)

> "Now if your right eye is snaring you, wrench it out and cast it from you, for it is expedient for you that one of your members should perish and not your whole body be cast into Gehenna." (Matthew 5:29)

Speaking of the futuristic kingdom, the prophet Isaiah fortells:

> "For as the new heavens and the new earth, which I will make, shall remain before me, saith the Lord, so shall your seed and your name remain. And it shall come to pass, that from one new moon to another, and from one sabbath to another, shall all flesh come to worship before me, saith the Lord. And they shall go forth, and look upon the carcases of the men that have transgressed against me: for their worm shall not die, neither shall their fire be quenched; and they shall be an abhorring unto all flesh." (Isaiah 66:22-24 KJV)

Note that "all flesh" shall see the corpses of these "mortals" burning in the fire as they come to Jerusalem to worship during the reign of Christ. Compare this with the last few chapters of Revelation, where we see the fulfillment of this prophesy. This is not the spiritual "heaven," but a very physical "kingdom." And outside this physical "New Jerusalem" will be a place called the "Valley of Hinnom," or "Gehenna," which is the physical place Jesus speaks of.

Those hearing Jesus' words as He spoke would have been quite disturbed about the possibility of being cast into Gehenna. For a Jew to be denied a proper burial would be shameful. To have one's body cast into Gehenna, this refuse dump outside Jerusalem, would be a disgrace.

TARTARUS

The Greek word "Tartarus" is used only once in Scripture (2 Peter 2:4):

> "For if God spares not sinning messengers, but thrusting them into the gloomy caverns of ***Tartarus***, gives them up to be kept for chastening judging…"

This place "Tartarus," then, is a place where sinning messengers (angels) are kept as they await the judgment. It does not refer to a place where men are sent at all, nor does it speak of a final destination where there is everlasting torment. It is a temporary place reserved for sinning messengers...period!

"HELL"

Part of the problem, then, is that one Hebrew word and three different Greek words (with three very distinct meanings) have been carelessly combined into a single word "hell," to create our present-day image of "hell."

It is interesting to look at our English word "hell" for a moment. This word "helan," of Anglo Saxon origin, had an original meaning of "to cover up" or "to hide," much like what we have seen "sheol" and "hades" really mean. The variations "hele", "helle", "hell", "heile" and "helan" can be found. In some parts of England the word is still used to mean something that is covered over.

Some common English words, like "helmet" (to cover one's head), have come from the root "helle."

LAKE OF FIRE

Besides the various Hebrew and Greek words translated "hell," the "Lake of Fire" is referred to five times in Scripture. Only two of these refer to a conscious torment, and in both of these cases no humans are included in the description.

> Revelation 19:20 "And the wild beast is arrested, and with it the false prophet who does the signs in its sight, by which he deceives those getting the emblem of the wild beast, and those worshiping its image. Living, the two were cast into the *__lake of fire__* burning with sulphur."

> Revelation 20:10 "And the Adversary who is deceiving them was cast into the *__lake of fire__* and sulphur, where the wild beast and where the false prophet are also. And they shall be tormented day and night for the eons of the eons."

In these instances only the wild beast (Adversary/Satan) and the false prophet are cast into the lake of fire, and as we learned in the previous chapter they will be tormented not forever and ever, but for the eons (at least two) of the eons.

> Revelation 20:13-15 "And the sea gives up the dead in it, and death and the unseen (hades) give up the dead in them. And they were condemned, each in accord with their acts. And death and the unseen were cast into the ***lake of fire***. This is the second death—the ***lake of fire***. And if anyone was not found written in the scroll of life, he was cast into the ***lake of fire***."

> Revelation 21:7-8 "To him who is thirsting I shall be giving of the spring of the water of life gratuitously. He who is conquering shall be enjoying this allotment, and I shall be a God to him and he shall be a son to Me. Yet the timid, and unbelievers, and the abominable, and murderers, and paramours, and enchanters, and idolaters, and all the false— their part is in the ***lake of burning*** with fire and sulphur, which is the second death."

In these cases referring to humans being cast into the lake of fire,

1. No duration is mentioned, and
2. In both cases the lake of fire is further described as "the second death."

Based on this description I would say two possibilities exist. We have already seen that "death" is simply a dissolution, or a dis-assembly of the body and spirit, with the body returned to the earth and the spirit returning to God. The soul is in "hades" which is "the unseen" place. Do we have reason to assume that the second death will be any different? We have seen that only the "unhuman" Adversary/beast and the false prophet will be ***tormented*** for the eons of the eons. No similar mention is made of humans cast into the lake of fire. It may be as simple as their being put to death once again, forfeiting the allotment of "eonian life" which is granted to Believers.

In death once again, they await the "consummation" that Paul speaks of in 1 Corinthians 15 which will occur at the end of the eons when God becomes All in all.

Some may object and say that these creatures being cast into the lake of fire are unworthy and unfit to spend eternity with God in the heavens, even at the end of the ages after having experienced the second death. I would contend that none of us who have confessed Jesus Christ as our Lord and Saviour are ready either. It is only because of the work of Jesus Christ that we are "made ready" to spend eternity with God in the heavens. We fall far short, as do those who have not yet confessed Jesus Christ as Saviour. As we look at the fallen nature even within the Body of Christ today (and in the days of the Corinthian believers) we see that only the incorruptible bodies received at the resurrection (1 Corinthians 15) will enable us to live incorruptible lives in heaven.

The other possibility relative to the lake of fire is a conscious period of "refinement," as God prepares those affected for the grand consummation of history as found in 1 Corinthians 15. We are not given a great deal of information about the lake of fire, so this is simply conjecture. But consider the following.

1. "Fire" is the Greek "pur," from which our English words purify and purge come.

2. God's use of fire to purify, instead of to torment, is much more consistent with His character of love.

3. God appeared to Moses in the form of a burning bush (Exodus 3), from which Moses hid his face.

Could it be that the lake of fire is the very presence of God (as when God appeared to Moses), purifying and refining instead of tormenting?

Consider the following passages:

> Jeremiah 9:6-7 "You live in the midst of deception; in their deceit they refuse to acknowledge me, declares the Lord. Therefore this is what the Lord Almighty says: See I will ___*refine and test*___ them, for what else can I do because of the sin of my people?" (NIV)

> Malachi 3:2-3 "But who can endure the day of his coming? Who can stand when he appears? For he will be like a ___*refiner's fire*___ or a launderer's soap. He will sit as a ___*refiner and purifier*___ of silver; he will ___*purify*___ the Levites and ___*refine*___ them like gold and silver." (NIV)

I could never understand how God, who is a God of love, could torment in fire forever those who did not accept Jesus Christ as Saviour in this short lifetime. I can fully understand the lake of fire if its purpose (refinement and purification) is consistent with the love of God, with the ultimate goal of saving all creation at the end of the ages.

I do not question that there is a judgment; surely there is! I do not question that there is a lake of fire! But the Bible tells us that the lake of fire is the second death, and it is not eternal but will one day be abolished. (1 Corinthians 15) If we teach that God will punish men eternally for what they have done during this brief lifetime, it is to charge God with injustice.

THE NATURE OF JUDGMENT AND PUNISHMENT

Dr. David Hartley, a proponent of Universalism who was born in 1705, reasoned:

> "The evils that befall us here have a tendency to promote our good. Analogy teaches that the evils of another life will have a like good effect...The infinite goodness of God is manifestly

56

an argument in favor of Universal Salvation." ("The Modern History of Universalism," page 219)

The Greek "krino" and "krisis" are properly translated "judge" or "judgment." This is a neutral term, simply signifying that one's case has been reviewed and determined by the Righteous Judge. It does not in and of itself designate the nature of the punishment. But the KJV renders these words in a variety of ways, clearly not all relaying the same meaning:

Judgment, damnation, condemnation, accusation, avenge

A passage often used to "prove" an eternal hell is the separation of sheep and goats event described in Matthew 25:46,

"And these shall go away into **everlasting punishment:** but the righteous into life eternal." (KJV)

"Everlasting punishment" is "kolasin aionion" in the Greek. William Barclay, well known Greek scholar, professor and author of the popular Bible commentary "The Daily Study Bible Series" (Westminster Press) says:

"The Greek word for punishment is kolasis, which was not originally an ethical word at all. It originally meant the pruning of trees to make them grow better. I think it is true to say that in all Greek secular literature kolasis is never used of anything but remedial punishment." (page 66, "William Barclay, A Spiritual Autobiography")

Michael Phillips quotes from a letter he received from William Barclay as a part of his compiling "Universal Reconciliation, A Brief Selection of Pertinent Quotations" (Sunrise Books):

"...there is no instance in Greek where kolasis does not mean remedial punishment. This would enable us to argue that God's punishment is always for man's cure...It is the simple fact that in Greek kolasis always means a remedial punishment." (page 84)

On the same page, Phillips also quotes A. R. Symonds:

"The distinctive meaning of this word, kolasis is corrective punishment, being derived from a verb which means to prune. I say its distinctive meaning is this, in relation to another word, timoria, which signifies vindictive punishment."

In "Salvator Mundi, or Is Christ the Saviour of All Men?" by Samuel Cox, we read:

"The Greek has two words for 'punishment;' kolasis, the word used by our Lord, and timoria, a word also used in the New Testament (Heb 10:29): and the distinctive meanings of these two words are defined by Aristotle himself. The one word, that used by Christ, denotes, he says, that kind of punishment which is intended for the improvement of the offender; while the other denotes that kind of punishment which is intended for the vindication of law and justice. And even the advocates of endless torment admit that the word selected by Christ means, according to the Greek usage, remedial discipline, punishment designed to reform and improve men, to prune away their defects and sins." (page 141)

The distinction between "kolasis" and "timoria" is supported by the following passages where "timoria" is used:

Acts 22:5 Paul speaks of his past, when he led the believers to Jerusalem to be "***punished***."

Acts 26:11 Paul again speaks of his persecution and "***punishment***" of the believers.

Hebrew 10:29 Speaks of the "***punishment***" that would be *deserved* by one who "tramples on the Son of God."

John Wesley Hanson writes in "The Greek Word Aion-Aionios,"

> "All God's punishments are those of a Father, and must therefore be adopted to the improvement of his children." (pg 50)

In Job 5:17-18 we read:

> "Behold, happy is the man whom God correcteth; therefore despise not thou the chastening of the Almighty. For he maketh sore, and bindeth up; he woundeth, and his hands make whole." (KJV)

The argument was introduced by Augustine that if "aionios kolasis" did not mean "endless punishment" then there is no assurance for the believer that "aionios zoe" means "endless life." It is very interesting to note that it was not until the 5th century A.D. that theologians began for the first time to introduce the sense of endlessness, rather than eonian (or age-abiding) which had been the interpretation prior to that time.

It seems, then, that the new meanings for the words "aionian" and "kolasis" crept in out of a fear that eternal life could not be supported unless there was also eternal punishment. And if punishment was eternal it could not be corrective in nature, so it must be vengeful. As a result, we have come to associate the passages referring to judgment as punishment to repay for past wrongs. Instead God's Word refers to judgment as a correction, chastisement or discipline.

For example, Matthew 25:46 reads:

> "And these shall go away into everlasting punishment: but the righteous into life eternal." (KJV)

This verse is translated in the CLNT:

> "And these shall be coming away into chastening eonian, yet the just into life eonian."

Rotherham's Emphasized Bible translates this passage:

> "And these shall go away into age-abiding correction, but the righteous into age-abiding life."

God has always stressed the importance of forgiveness:

> "Yet if your brother should be sinning, rebuke him, and if he should ever indeed repent, forgive him. And if he should ever be sinning against you seven times a day, and if he should ever be turning about seven times a day to you, saying, 'I am repenting,' you shall be forgiving him." (Matthew 17:3-4)

> "Then, approaching, Peter said to Him, 'Lord, how many times shall my brother be sinning against me and I shall be pardoning him? Till seven times?' Jesus is saying to him, 'I am not saying to you Till seven times, but Till seventy times and seven.'" (Matthew 18:21-22)

Of the lost ones, Jesus said:

> "What man of you, having a hundred sheep, and losing one of them, is not leaving the ninety-nine in the wilderness and is going after the lost one, *till he may be finding it?*" (Luke 15:3)

How can one be chastised and corrected if the punishment lasts forever? How can God, who places such emphasis on forgiveness, come to the point where He refuses to forgive? How can God, who places importance on the one lost sheep, be satisfied if **_all_** the sheep are not securely in the fold when all is said and done?

Does it not make better sense that the purpose of judgment is for correction, in preparation for a future day when every knee shall bow before Him? Is this not more consistent with God's character of love and forgiveness?

Could God really be filled with love and power and wisdom, and yet be unable or unwilling to find a way to bring the necessary correction to every one of His creation, in order that every knee bows before Him?

Consider the facts.

Man was created through no act of his own,
but only through the will of God.
Man, in the Garden of Eden, was tempted by evil,
and God knew beforehand of man's being predisposed to evil.
In his short lifetime,
man is continually exposed to temptation.
But if man does not respond
by accepting Jesus Christ as his Saviour
in this **short lifetime,**
he is consigned to an **eternal torment in hell.**

Is this logical? Does it not place a great emphasis on the ability of man to see through his depravity, and to overcome the temptation all around him, to make a "decision for Christ?"

If an earthly ruler condemned even the vilest criminal to be kept alive just to be tortured forever, we would shudder at his cruelty. But we have inherited the current orthodox teachings about God that calmly attribute such activities to Him, while also teaching that He is a God of love.

I have come to see that the Bible does not teach this at all. Man has intervened and has placed his philosophies and pagan ideas within the Word of God. The modern English translations now perpetuate these man-made ideas, primarily because of a few words mis-translated and misinterpreted. We see a God of love, but a God who is also very harsh. Some say this is necessary because of God's holiness and justice, but is God not able to use His love and power to bring about justice without losing a single sheep from the fold?

61

SUMMARY

The penalty for sin is death.

Christ paid the penalty for sin on our behalf.

If the penalty for sin had been eternal torment, Christ would have had to pay that penalty.

The resurrection shows us that the penalty could not have been eternal torment, or
Christ would still be paying that price on our behalf.

If one dies without faith in Christ, he would be subject to the penalty for sin...death.
(This is the second death...the lake of fire.)

But because Christ overcame death, at the consummation (at the end of the ages)
death will be abolished, and those within the lake of fire (second death) will be
reconciled with God, who becomes All in all. (1 Corinthians 15)

STUDY FOR YOURSELF

I am not asking you to believe these things based on my opinions. I have presented some Biblical references in support of my arguments, but encourage you to study for yourself. In light of what I have told you, look at all of the occurrences of these key Hebrew and Greek words. Don't trust the modern English translators who have built their own biases into the translation. Throw off your previously biased images of "hell" and "judgment." Study these references for yourself.

SHEOL (65 occurrences) - KJV translation precedes each group of references
    Grave: Gen 37:35; Gen 42:38; Gen 44:29,31; 1 Sam 2:6; 1 Kings 2:6,9; Job 7:9; Job 14:13; Job 17:13; Job 21:13; Job 24:19; Psalm 6:5; Psalm 30:3; Psalm 31:17; Psalm 49:14,15; Psalm 88:3; Psalm 89:48; Psalm 141:7; Prov 1:12; Prov 30:16; Ecc 9:10; Song of Songs 8:6; Is 14:11; Is 38:10,18; Ezek 31:15; Hos 13:14.
    Hell: Deut 32:22; 2 Sam 22:6; Job 11:8; Job 26:6; Psalm 9:17; Psalm 16:10; Psalm 18:5; Psalm 55:15; Psalm 86:13; Psalm 116:3; Psalm 139:8; Prov 5:5; Prov 7:27; Prov 9:18; Prov 15:11,24; Prov 23:14; Prov 27:20; Is 5:14; Is 14:9,15; Is 28:15,18; Is 57:9; Ezek 31:16,17; Ezek 32:21,27; Amos 9:2; Jonah 2:2; Hab 2:5
    The Pit: Num 16:30,33; Job 17:16

HADES (11 occurrences)
    Hell: Matt 11:23; Matt 16:18; Luke 10:15; Luke 16:23; Acts 2:27,31; Rev 1:18; Rev 6:8; Rev 20:13,14.
    Grave: 1 Cor 15:55

GEHENNA (12 occurrences)
    Hell: Matt 5:22,29,30; Matt 10:28; Mat 18:9; Matt 23:15,33; Mark 9:43,45,47; Luke 12:5; James 3:6

TARTARUS (1 occurrence)
    Hell: 2 Peter 2:4

LAKE OF FIRE (5 occurrences)
    For wild beast, false prophet Satan: Rev 19:20; Rev 20:10
    For irreverant mankind: Rev 20:14,15; Rev 21:8

Chapter Six

ALL, OR JUST SOME?

The Bible contains many references to the salvation of **ALL**!

Because I had always been taught that some would not be saved, but would spend eternity in hell, I always found it necessary to restrict these "**ALL**" verses, even though the context does not make any restriction. If we do not restrict the "**ALL**," then there are contradictions within God's Word (as commonly translated), and this cannot be. We determine that because of eternal punishment, the "**ALL**" passages cannot really mean "**ALL**," but only "all who accept Jesus Christ as their Saviour in this lifetime." In other words we eliminate the contradictions within God's Word by placing **restrictions** on some passages.

But now we have seen that "aion" should not be translated "eternal," but "eon" (or "age"). And we have seen that "hell" as found in the Bible is not the place of eternal punishment we had been led to believe. And we have seen that God's "punishment" is really a remedial discipline, not to torment but to correct.

And so when the Bible uses the word "**ALL**" maybe that is exactly what is meant…"**ALL**" without any restriction whatsoever.

Let's look at some of these passages.

<u>CHRIST IS THE SAVIOUR OF ALL</u>
We read in 1 Timothy 4:9-11,

"we rely on the living God, Who is the Saviour of **all** mankind, **especially** of believers."

This passage clearly tells us that God is the Saviour of **ALL** mankind, not just believers! Some say that the word **ESPECIALLY** restricts the **ALL** to the believers. But this is clearly not what the writer is expressing, or he would have simply said that God is the Saviour of all who believe.

The word **ESPECIALLY** is "malista" in the Greek, and we also find it in Galations 6:10,

"Consequently, then, as we have occasion, we are working for the good of **all**, yet **specially** for the family of faith."

Do we interpret this verse to mean that we are not to work for the good of all, but **ONLY** for those within the family of faith? Certainly not! We are instructed to work for the good of **ALL**, and in a special way, or perhaps even giving a priority to, those within the family of faith.

Likewise when we read that God is the Saviour of **ALL**, and **ESPECIALLY** those who believe, we see that while God is truly the Saviour of **ALL**, there is something special or unique about those who believe in this present age. Certainly there is, for the believers are those who have, by faith, been saved already in receiving the evangel (gospel) in this lifetime. Their reward will be "eonian life" and not the second death. But there will come a time, at the end of the ages (as seen in 1 Corinthians 15) when death will be abolished and when God becomes All in all, and **ALL** will be saved.

GOD'S WILL, AND HIS OPERATIONS

We read in 1 Timothy 2:4,

"God, who wills that **all** mankind be saved and come into a realization of the truth."

Some will say that while it is God's **will** that all mankind be saved, since he has given us free will it may be possible that some will reject Him, and will not be saved. In other words, God's **will** cannot be realized because the will of mankind to reject Him, or the will of Satan to deceive, will overcome God's will to save all mankind.

Assuming we have free will (and that we do not simply think we have the ability to freely choose at every turn), consider this. When God created man, in that perfect Garden of Eden, evil was already present. Man did not even have the ability to exercise his free will on neutral ground, but was tempted and enticed by the serpent, who was also in the Garden.

Man disobeyed, and was expelled from the Garden. The consequence was the process of dying, leading ultimately to death. But Scripture tells us that God knew the cross would be necessary even "before the disruption of the world." (see 1 Peter 1:19-21) In other words, God knew man would sin, and death would enter the scene.

But what if God could, through the course of time (the "eons"), in His infinite wisdom and power and love, find a way to save **ALL** of mankind?

Consider the life of Joseph. He was mistreated by his brothers, sold into slavery, framed by Potiphar's wife, jailed...yet ultimately God used all of this to accomplish His purpose. Despite the free will of Joseph's brothers who sought to harm him, or Potiphar's wife who sought to frame him, or anyone else who may have entered Joseph's life; still God was able to accomplish His purpose.

> "And you, you devised against me evil, yet the Alueim (God) devises it for me for good, that it may work out as at this day, to preserve alive many people." Genesis 50:20 (CVOT)

God's purpose was to save His people when the famine struck (and in the process to save the Egyptians as well). He selected Joseph as His instrument. Despite the free will exercised by those who would thwart Joseph (or thwart God's will), God's will prevailed.

Consider Ephesians 1:11 which speaks of God as:

"The One Who is operating **all** in accord with the counsel of His will."

If it is God's will that **ALL** mankind is saved, and if God is truly operating **ALL** in accord with the counsel of His will, who can thwart His plan?

I think of the power of advertising, which has become a detailed science. Billions of dollars are spent on advertising, toward the objective of influencing our decisions. Advertising gives us the desire to buy things we didn't know we really needed or wanted. Our free will has not been removed, yet we often make decisions because of the influence of advertising.

If advertising executives can influence our free will in this way, why do we question God's ability to allow free will, but to ultimately bring all mankind to the point where He is recognized, and that every knee bows before Him?

CONTRAST BETWEEN ADAM AND CHRIST
There are a few instances in Scripture where Adam is directly contrasted with Christ.

"For since, in fact, through a man came death, through a Man, also, comes the resurrection of the dead. For even as, in Adam, *all are dying*, thus also, in Christ, shall *all be vivified*. Yet each in his own class..." 1 Corinthians 15:21-23

G. Campbell Morgan, preacher, teacher, evangelist, and "prince of expositors" says of this passage in his "The Corinthian Letters of Paul,"

"In the program of God all are to be made alive in Christ."

Does this tell us that **ALL** die in Adam, but only those accepting Jesus Christ as Saviour in this lifetime will live in Christ? Unless we restrict the **ALL** that die in Adam, how can we restrict the **ALL** who will live in Christ?

> "Consequently, then, as it was through one offense for *all mankind* for condemnation, thus also it is through one just award for *all mankind* for life's justifying. For even as, through the disobedience of the one man, the many were constituted sinners, thus also, through the obedience of the One, the many shall be constituted just." Romans 5:18-19

Again this is a direct comparison between Adam and Christ. If we could make a case that **ALL** did not die in Adam, we could make a case that **ALL** will not be constituted just. But there is nowhere in Scripture any limitation on those who die in Adam. Likewise there is no restriction found in Scripture that would limit salvation. The only limitation has been placed there by the mistranslation and misinterpretion of Scripture.

CHRIST'S PURPOSE
Consider the following passages:

> "Lo, the Lamb of God, which is taking away the sin of *the world*." (John 1:29)

> "One Mediator of God and mankind, a Man, Christ Jesus, Who is giving Himself a correspondent Ransom *for all*." (1 Timothy 2:6)

> "*Every* knee should be bowing...*every* tongue should be acclaiming" (Philippians 2:9 and Isaiah 45:23)

> "For even as you once were stubborn toward God, yet now were shown mercy at their stubbornness, thus these also are

68

now stubborn to this mercy of yours, that now they also may be shown mercy. For God locks up all together in stubbornness, that He should be merciful to *all*." (Romans 11:30-32)

Where is the restriction on the **ALL** or **EVERY** in these verses? Again, we have placed the restriction there in our thinking, so as to reconcile these passages with those that talk about eternal condemnation. But once we recognize that there are no Biblical references that teach eternal condemnation (but only age-abiding correction), we can see these wonderful passages for what they really are.

"I, if I should be exalted out of the earth, shall be drawing *all* to Myself." John 12:32

William Barclay, respected teacher and commentator, says of this passage:

"The word all means all. It is not possible for the word all to mean anything else, but all. Part of the trouble in the interpretation of Scripture is the refusal of people to take it at its face value which is nearly always right." (From "Universal Reconciliation, a Brief Selection of Pertinent Quotations" compiled by Michael Phillips, page 26. This quotation came from a letter directed to Mr. Phillips by William Barclay.)

I am in no way mitigating Christ's work upon the cross. Christ's death and subsequent resurrection were very necessary in order for us to be granted salvation. The only question is the **scope** of Christ's work upon the cross. Does it have effect only for those who believe upon Him in this lifetime, or will there come a day when **ALL** are saved by His work upon the cross?

ALL CREATION RECONCILED
Consider very carefully Colossians 1:16-20,

"for in Him is **all created**, that in the heavens and that on the earth, the visible and the invisible, whether thrones, or lordships, or sovereignties, or authorities, all is created through Him and for Him, and He is before all, and all has its cohesion in Him. And He is the Head of the body, the ecclesia, Who is Sovereign, Firstborn from among the dead, that in all He may be becoming first, for in Him the entire complement delights to dwell, and through Him *to reconcile all* to Him (making peace through the blood of His cross), through Him, whether those on the earth or those in the heavens."

ALL is created through Him, and **ALL** is reconciled. Consider the global nature of this passage. **ALL CREATION** is included...visible and invisible. He is the firstborn from among the dead. In Him the entire complement delights to dwell (the Body of Christ...those believing in this present age). And through Him **ALL** is reconciled.

THE CONSUMMATION

When will the salvation of all take place? We look to 1 Corinthians 15:21-28,

"For since, in fact, through a man came death, through a Man, also, comes the resurrection of the dead. For even as, in Adam, all are dying, thus also, in Christ, shall all be vivified. Yet each in his own class: the Firstfruit, Christ; thereupon those who are Christ's in His presence; thereafter *the consummation*, whenever He may be giving up the kingdom to His God and Father, whenever He should be nullifying all sovereignty and all authority and power. For He must be reigning until He should be placing all His enemies under His feet. The last enemy is being abolished: death. For He subjects all under His feet. Now whenever He may be saying that all is subject, it is evident that it is outside of Him Who subjects all to Him. Now, whenever all may be subjected to Him, then the Son Himself also shall be subjected to Him Who subjects all to Him, that God may be All in all."

This is the grand conclusion of the ages. God has taken what mankind (and Satan) have intended for evil, and He has used it to achieve good. He has operated all in accord with the counsel of His will to achieve His will...that **ALL** mankind be saved. Some have recognized the greatness of God, and the work of the Saviour, in this lifetime, by faith. Others have taken longer, but now find salvation also. Every knee is now bowing in subjection before Him. Every person has found salvation. Every lost sheep has been found. The purpose of the eons has been achieved, and God is now All in all.

IS THIS TOO DIFFICULT FOR GOD?

Thomas Allin states in his "Christ Triumphant" (page 1),

"All forms of partial salvation are but so many different ways of saying that evil is in the long run too strong for God."

Through the work of Christ upon the Cross, Believers agree that God has provided for the salvation of sinners. The difference is that the "orthodox" belief is that this salvation applies only to those who believe in this lifetime. Is God unable to overcome the evil that exists within the many others of His creation?

THINK FOR YOURSELF

Like me, you have probably been taught to restrict the "**ALL**" passages. But consider the things we have discussed in this chapter. Read the Bible with this new "lens," this new possibility. Is it possible that God will ultimately save ALL? Study. Think for yourself.

Chapter Seven

PUTTING IT ALL TOGETHER

We have looked at various facts that seem to point toward an ultimate reconciliation of all, but how do the events described in the Bible fit together? You may have considered and even studied much of God's Word, but have you seen God working since the eons began, moving deliberately toward a happy conclusion when all are reconciled to Him?

As we read the Word of God from beginning to end we can see God working systematically through the ages, and we see Him revealing to mankind His plan in bits and pieces. Some information He revealed to the patriarchs in the Old Testament. Some things He revealed through His prophets. Some things He revealed through Christ Jesus. But some things were concealed until God was ready to reveal them through His servant Paul, after the Jews had been set aside so that the complement of Gentiles could be incorporated into the fold.

Studying individual portions of God's Word is like analyzing a tree, and we can learn many marvelous things about the tree in this way. But sometimes we must step back to look at the entire forest, to see how all of the trees fit together to comprise the forest.

Let us now step back from the beautiful trees for a few moments, to examine this wonderful forest which is God's Word, and to see how God has worked and is working through the eons, or ages.

GARDEN OF EDEN

Genesis describes the beginning of mankind in the Garden of Eden. It is interesting that despite this being a Paradise where Adam and Eve lived in the presence of God, and where there would be no death, evil existed even in this place. The serpent lived in their midst, and had access to Adam and Eve so as to tempt them. This was not a neutral setting, where Adam and Eve would simply live in obedience to God. The evil one lived among them, and tempted them.

What an interesting parallel to Jesus who was led by God to the wilderness ***to be tempted*** by the Adversary. (Matthew 4:1) Adam and Eve are "led" by God to the Garden of Eden ***to be tempted*** by the serpent. The difference is the outcome. Adam and Eve succumb to the temptation, and death enters the world. Jesus overcomes the temptation, and defeats death. Paul later makes the same comparison, and reveals to us the impact of these events. As in Adam all are dying, thus also in Christ will all live. (1 Corinthians 15:22)

MANKIND DETERIORATES

Once expelled from the Garden, mankind follows a steady course of self-destruction. Cain kills Abel. Evil runs rampant. In Genesis 6 we start over, with the wicked being destroyed and only the righteous Noah and his family surviving. But we read on, and mankind continues to show no promise. At Babel (Genesis 11) God finds it necessary to confuse the tongues of mankind, and scatter them.

GOD CHOOSES ONE MAN, TO BLESS ALL PEOPLE

From all of mankind God chooses one man, Abram (later Abraham), promising to bless all people on the earth through him. (Genesis 12:3) We see here God's purpose or intent: To bless all people upon the earth. His method at this point is to choose one man, Abram, as His instrument (or channel) to bless all people.

Later God chooses a descendant of Abraham, Jacob. He repeats His promise to bless all people through Jacob. (Genesis 28:14) God later re-names Jacob "Israel." (Genesis 32)

GOD'S PURPOSES PREVAIL

Joseph becomes the central figure in Genesis 37. He is sold into slavery, framed by Potiphar's wife, thrown into jail, and forgotten. But God continues to raise Joseph up, and he eventually becomes the second most powerful man in Egypt, directly beneath Pharoah. At the end of Genesis Joseph's brothers stand before him after their father had died, and they fear what Joseph might do to them. They remember how they had plotted against Joseph and sold him into slavery years before.

Joseph says to them, "You intended to harm me, but God intended it for good, to accomplish what is now being done, the saving of many lives." (Genesis 50:19) God had purposed to "save many lives," knowing that famine was coming to the land. He accomplished his purpose through Joseph. Nothing that was done to Joseph by his brothers, by Potiphar's wife, or by any in Egypt…could prevent God's purpose from being accomplished.

GOD CHOOSES A NATION

In Exodus 1:6 we read that the descendents of Jacob (Israel) are now "The Israelites." Through the remainder of the Old Testament God will use the Israelites, His people, to accomplish His purposes. Remember God's promise to Jacob; to bless all people through him. Now Jacob's descendents will be used for this purpose.

God does not choose Israel to show favoritism, or even because the Israelites are better than the non-Israelites. As God's plan continues to unfold we will see how He uses Israel, the nation, as His instrument to ultimately bless all nations.

THE KINGDOM

In 2 Samuel the Israelites become a powerful nation under David's reign, and the success of the nation continues under the reign of his son, Solomon. But at Solomon's death the nation divides. The northern kingdom (Israel) and the southern kingdom (Judah) have a series of kings as reported in 1 & 2 Kings and 1 & 2 Chronicles. Some kings are wicked, instituting or condoning the worship of idols and other evil practices. Other kings are good, bringing reform and a return to the ways of God.

EXILE

The prophets of God warn the people that if they do not turn from their wicked ways and return to God, their land will be taken from them. Israel is more wicked than Judah, and is the first to be taken from the land. (2 Kings 17) Judah goes on a bit longer, but is later defeated and taken away into exile. (2 Kings 25) Sin and disobedience have resulted in exile. As Adam and Eve were once expelled from the Garden because of their disobedience, so also the nation of Israel suffers the same fate.

THE PROPHETS

While in exile, a common message of the prophets is, "Return to God." There are promises brought by the prophets to the exiled nation. The scattered people will one day be returned to their land. (see Ezekiel 28:25) After a season of punishment, Israel will be restored. We see this "restoration" promised in Joel 2:18; Hosea 14; Amos 9:11; and Zephaniah 3:9.

Habakkuk 2:14 points to a day in the future when the earth will be filled with the knowledge of the glory of the Lord.

Daniel promises a new kingdom in the future; one that will come from heaven and be more powerful than all earthly kingdoms. (Daniel 2:44)

RETURN TO THE LAND

As promised, the scattered Israelites are returned to the land. We read in Ezra of the Temple being re-built. Nehemiah tells of the rebuilding of the walls of Jerusalem.

AWAITING THE MESSIAH

As the New Testament opens, the people are back in the land, but they are under Roman rule. While a part of the promise of the prophets has been fulfilled, more is to come. The people are awaiting the Messiah, the Son of God. They are looking for the days of David and Solomon to return, when the kingdom was strong and the people safe. The Old Testament prophets had foretold that a kingdom like this would be coming, so the people waited.

PUNISHMENT FOR SIN IN THE OLD TESTAMENT

In Genesis we learned that the penalty for sin was death. Throughout the Old Testament we witness this time and again. Destruction (death) is the lot of the wicked. Ultimately since all sin, death is the lot of all.

It is interesting that throughout all of the Old Testament we read of death and destruction, but never "eternal hell" as a punishment for those who sin. The sole penalty for sin is death.

THE KINGDOM IS NEAR

As the people await the Messiah and the kingdom, how wonderful it is to hear from John the Baptist, "Near is the kingdom of the heavens." (Matthew 3:1) Remember the prophets of old had said to the people, "Return to God, and He will restore you." Now John is saying the same thing: "Repent, for near is the kingdom of the heavens." But the Jewish leaders are skeptical of John, or perhaps they feel that no repentance is necessary on their part.

When Jesus begins preaching, he proclaims the same message: "Repent, for near is the kingdom of the heavens." (Matthew 4:17) Multitudes follow Jesus, and as He talks of the coming kingdom His message is accompanied by many signs and wonders. But the Jewish leaders reject Jesus, and ultimately crucify Him.

THE KINGDOM IS PREACHED IN ACTS

The "kingdom message" is re-introduced in Acts, with Peter now the central figure. Jesus had promised that the keys to the kingdom would be given to Peter (Matthew 16:19) and this happens in Acts, as signs and wonders accompany Peter's proclamation of the coming kingdom. And, as was the case with the preaching of Jesus, the "kingdom message" is going to the Jews, not the Gentiles.

Peter proclaims to the Jews,

> "Repent, then, and turn about for the erasure of your sins, so that seasons of refreshing should be coming from the face of the Lord, and He should dispatch the One fixed upon before you, Christ Jesus, Whom heaven must indeed receive until the times of restoration of all which God speaks through the mouth of His holy prophets who are from the eon." Acts 3:19-21

This message is very similar to that of John the Baptist and of Jesus Himself. Repentance is called for. But Peter is tying the return of the kingdom to this repentance. "Repent," he says, "so that Christ Jesus comes, and seasons of refreshing will come."

In response to Peter's proclamation, had the "sheep of Israel" repented, Christ Jesus would have come and the kingdom would have been established. But throughout Acts, while the kingdom message is received by some, it is rejected by others. As the kingdom is continually rejected, God begins to move among the Gentiles. Peter is hesitant, but eventually goes as prompted by God to Cornelius, a God fearing Gentile. (Acts 10)

Peter and his Jewish companions are "amazed" when the holy spirit falls on those Gentiles hearing the word. (Acts 10:44) They are not expecting God to work among the Gentiles as He had among the Jews. They had forgotten that God's plan is to bless all people through the Jews, who are acting as God's instruments to accomplish this purpose.

SAUL (PAUL)

In Acts 9, as Saul travels to Damascus to continue his persecution of the Believers, the risen Jesus appears to him. Saul is chosen as Christ's instrument to bear His name "before both the nations and kings, besides the sons of Israel..." (Acts 9:15-16) Paul is the first, then, to be specifically commissioned to go to the Gentiles ("nations and kings"), although he is also commissioned to go to the "sons of Israel" as had John the Baptist, Jesus and Peter.

ELYMAS (BAR-JESUS) & SERGIUS PAUL

One of the first incidents we read about in Saul's ministry is the encounter with Elymas, the Magician, also known as Bar-Jesus, in Acts 13. Sergius Paul, a proconsul who is an intelligent man (a Gentile), calls for Saul and Barnabas. Sergius Paul asks to hear the word of God, but Elymas the Magician "withstood them, seeking to pervert the proconsul from the faith." Saul chastises Elymas for "perverting the straight ways of the Lord," and Elymas is blinded, "not observing the sun *until the appointed time*." The proconsul becomes a Believer.

Here, for the first time, we see that Saul "is also Paul." (Acts 13:9) Saul is a Hebrew name, while Paul is Greek. It is interesting that we are told of Saul's new Gentile name at the precise point where a Jew attempts to stop the word of God from going to a Gentile.

Also interesting are the words spoken to Elymas when he is blinded "*until the appointed time.*" This is very similar to Paul's explanation in Romans 11:25 that the callousness of Israel has come "*until the complement of the nations may be entering,*" after which time all Israel shall be saved. The incident with Elymas seems to be a picture of God's plan to set aside (or blind) Israel, for a time, while the word goes to the Gentiles.

PAUL BECOMES THE CENTRAL FIGURE IN ACTS

Remember Paul has received a dual commission. He is to go to the "nations and kings" and to the "sons of Israel." As he travels Paul generally goes first to the synagogues. He gathers some believers, but others reject him and even attempt to kill him.

Peter, who had been the primary figure in the early part of Acts begins to fade, and Paul becomes the primary figure after the incident with Elymas.

REJECTION BY THE JEWS; SALVATION TO THE NATIONS

Throughout the remainder of Acts we read of the persecution of Paul by the Jews who reject his message. Finally in Acts 28:17 Paul calls together the "foremost of the Jews." Some are persuaded, but others disbelieve. (Acts 28:24-25) As they disagree with one another, Paul concludes the book of Acts with these words:

> "Let it be known to you, then, that to the nations was dispatched this salvation of God, and they will hear." Acts 28:28

The final two verses in Acts report that Paul remains in Rome for two years, welcoming all who come to him. He heralds the kingdom of God, and teaches "that which concerns the Lord Jesus Christ." We learn what he taught as we read the letters of Paul, from Romans through Philemon.

PAUL'S MESSAGE NOT JUST A CONTINUATION OF PETER'S

We err when we think there is just one "Gospel." I was always taught that when we read the word "Gospel" in the Bible it is always the same. When we define "The Gospel" it is a compilation of every occurrence of the word in the entire New Testament. But this is mixing together things that are different.

"Gospel" comes from the Greek "evangel." It simply means "good news." This is made clear from Luke 1:19 where the "evangel" is brought by Gabriel to Zechariah, and it is the good news concerning the coming birth of John the Baptist.

Throughout Matthew the "evangel" concerns the coming kingdom. But as the kingdom is rejected, could the "evangel" have changed? First the "evangel" went only to the Jews, who awaited their kingdom. Peter caused quite a stir when he took the "evangel" to Cornelius, a Gentile. They were all quite amazed when the holy spirit fell upon these Gentiles who heard.

When Paul went to take the "evangel" to the proconsul (a Gentile), Elymas (a Jew) tried to stop him.

But it is not just a difference of **_who_** the "evangel" is being preached to! It is a different message.

"MY EVANGEL"

There are several instances where Paul refers to the evangel as "*my* evangel." Why does he use this terminology? Is there not just one evangel...*the* evangel?

In Romans 2:16 Paul says,

> "God will be judging the hidden things of humanity, according to *my* evangel, through Jesus Christ."

Here Paul is speaking of the nations, not of the Jews who are awaiting a restoration of their kingdom. It is a different topic; a different message; a different evangel.

In Romans 16:25-26 Paul again refers to "*my* evangel," and here he makes reference to

> "the revelation of a *secret hushed in times eonian, yet manifested now…*"

Could Paul's "evangel," then, contain new information from God not previously revealed by the prophets of old, or by John the Baptist, or even by Jesus Himself?

Paul tells us in Galations 1:11 that this evangel he brings

> "is not in accord with man. For neither did I accept it from a man, nor was I taught it, but it came through a revelation of Jesus Christ."

If Paul's "evangel" is simply a continuation of the same "evangel" being proclaimed by Peter, why would Paul have not simply studied under Peter and the other apostles? In Galations he feels it is important to tell us that he did not get his evangel from any man, but through a *revelation* of Jesus Christ.

In Galations 2:7 Paul makes the distinction between the evangel "of the Uncircumcision" and the evangel "of the Circumcision." Grammatically, the genitive case is used, and not the dative case. This means that the proper translation is not the evangel _to_ the Circumcision or Uncircumcision, but the evangel _of_ the Circumcision or Uncircumcision. The distinction is not made between the recipient of the evangel. Instead, the distinction is made in the evangel itself. Paul has been entrusted with the evangel "of the Uncircumcision" and Peter is entrusted with the evangel "of the Circumcision."

We struggle with this distinction today, and try to blend the messages together into one "Gospel." This is exactly what those in

Peter's day tried to do. It is the reason they challenged Paul for not requiring circumcision of the Gentile believers. They had a hard time understanding that God was doing a new thing, which is why Paul found it necessary to explain that his evangel came not from men, but was a revelation from God, and it was a different evangel!

GEHENNA

If we fail to see this distinction, we blend together things that are different as we proclaim "The Gospel." When Jesus is talking about the kingdom which is to come, and when He talks about Gehenna (most often translated "hell") as the fate of those being punished for their crimes in the kingdom, we see the need to "spiritualize" the kingdom and Gehenna because we think it is all part of the same message. Whereas Jesus was talking about the physical fate of those deserving punishment in the physical kingdom, we have come to see Gehenna as an eternal hell for Unbelievers. But in doing so we ourselves have become unbelievers...at least to the extent that we do not believe from God's Word that there is still a kingdom to come **upon this earth**, with Christ reigning upon the throne.

IS THE KINGDOM STILL TO COME?

Is an earthly kingdom still to come? Just before Christ ascended into heaven He is asked by His followers, "Art Thou at this time restoring the kingdom to Israel?" (Acts 1:6) The Lord does not chastise them for missing the point. He does not tell them an earthly kingdom is not to come. Instead He tells them, "Not yours is it to know times or eras which the Father has placed in His own jurisdiction."

The kingdom is still to come. But Israel has been hardened "until the complement of the nations may be entering. And thus all Israel shall be saved..." (Romans 11:25)

THE BOOK OF REVELATION

The Book of Revelation is an unveiling of the kingdom that will one day come upon the earth. It is the kingdom in all of its fullness that was foretold by the prophets. The Jews had been hardened for a time, until the complement of the nations enters the ecclesia (the "called-out ones" – generally translated "church"). But now the time has come for "all Israel to be saved." Romans 11:26

So Christ does return, and the kingdom of the heavens as prophesied by Daniel and proclaimed by Christ now comes upon the earth.

> "And loud voices occurred in heaven, saying, 'The kingdom of this world became our Lord's and His Christ's, and He shall be reigning for the eons of the eons! Amen!" Revelation 11:15

But even through the very end of Revelation the kingdom is for the Jews. The nations are blessed through Israel, but Israel is prominent.

But a part of Paul's message was that "there is no distinction between Jew and Greek…" (Romans 10:12) In Ephesians 2:11-22 Paul tells us of this new thing God has done. Here he says that the nations were once, "in that era,"

1. ***Apart*** from Christ
2. ***Alienated*** from the citizenship of Israel
3. ***Guests*** of the promise covenants
4. Having ***no expectation***

But now:

1. Christ ***razes the barrier***
2. He makes the two (Jew/Gentile) into ***one new humanity***
3. He reconciles both into ***one body***

83

The rejection of the kingdom by the Jews seems to defeat God's purposes, but God's will cannot be thwarted. The rejection of the kingdom evangel has resulted in the Gentiles being brought into the ecclesia...the Body of Christ. Like Joseph's rejection by his brothers which eventually led to the fulfilling of God's purposes, now Israel's rejection has ultimately been used by God to accomplish His purposes.

REMOVE PAUL

To help us understand Paul's function as God's chosen instrument, let us remove him from the scene for a moment. In the classic movie "It's a Wonderful Life" the viewer (and George Bailey) is shown what would have happened in Bedford Falls had Bailey never been born. What if Paul had never been born, or what if he had been judged and destroyed for persecuting and killing the early Believers?

Without Paul, our Bible would contain 13 fewer books. We would jump from Acts to Hebrews. The kingdom that was foretold by the Old Testament prophets and proclaimed in Matthew through Acts would have come more quickly. There is no setting aside of Israel until the complement of Gentiles comes in, which Paul spoke of. The Gentiles are only blessed indirectly through the nation of Israel.

But if there is no delay for the sake of the Gentiles, there is also no need for Hebrews through Jude, which were letters directed to the scattered Jewish believers (those who had received the evangel of the Circumcision), as they awaited the kingdom. We lose 8 more books from our Bible.

The kingdom which was preached by Christ, and which was later proclaimed by Peter and the other apostles after the resurrection in Acts, now comes in Revelation. As Revelation ends we have the Jewish kingdom restored, and the nations are blessed through Israel.

Christ reigns upon the throne. Satan is in the lake of fire. Those whose names were not found written in the scroll of life have also been cast into the lake of fire.

Without Paul, this is where things end. At least this is the extent of God's plans that would have been revealed to us, if Paul had not been given more revelation to be shared.

ADD PAUL

George Bailey is brought back to reality. His mouth is bleeding, his clothes are wet, and Zuzu's petals are back in his pocket (my apologies to those who have never seen this movie).

Paul did live! Paul did see the risen Lord on the road to Damascus, as undeserving as he was. God did reveal things to Paul, which he shared with us in *his* evangel.

There is no difference between Jew and Gentile, as both are on equal standing as joint heirs. Just as in Adam *all* died, so also in Christ shall *all* be made alive. Through one offense for *all* mankind for condemnation (Adam), thus also it is through one just award (Christ) for *all* mankind for life's justifying. It is God's will that *all* men are saved. God is operating *all* in accord with the counsel of His will. Christ is the Saviour of *all* mankind, especially (but not exclusively) of believers.

But if the book ends with the lake of fire burning, how can these things come to pass?

When we read a book we are used to events that flow chronologically as we read. But the Bible is not an ordinary book. The end of all things is not found in Revelation, for God showed things to Paul which had been secrets in the past, but which were revealed to him. Things were revealed to Paul which were not revealed to John, the writer of Revelation.

As John was given the revelation he recorded which is found at the end of our Bible, he was shown the events upon the earth as the promised kingdom was instituted. As Daniel had prophesied, it was a kingdom which was greater than any previous kingdom. Christ Himself is upon the throne. The righteous live, and the wicked are punished.

But it is within Paul's writings that we are told what will happen even beyond the events of Revelation.

THE CONSUMMATION

As Revelation comes to an end, we see the end of the ages. But as the last "Amen" of Revelation 22 is uttered, there is more to come. The crowning event of the ages is found in 1 Corinthians 15, the "consummation" of the ages. Here God reveals what happens when the ages have concluded.

Many believe the end of Revelation is a description of the eternal heavens that we will experience when the resurrection takes place. But there are a number of reasons to conclude that this is not the case, and that 1 Corinthians 15 happens after the end of Revelation 22.

In Revelation 21:1 John perceives "a new heaven and a new earth," and he sees "the holy city, new Jerusalem, descending *out of heaven*…" The New Jerusalem is not heaven itself, but it descends *out of heaven*.

Revelation	1 Corinthians
22:5 The slaves of God are reigning	15:24 All sovereignty,
21:24 There are still "kings of	authority and power
the earth"	are nullified.
21:5 Christ is seated on the throne	15:25 Christ must reign *until* He places all enemies under his feet.

86

15:28 When all is subject to Christ, Christ subjects Himself to God.
15:24 All sovereignty, authority and power nullified.

21:8 Lake of fire (second death) still exists

15:27 Last enemy (death) abolished.

22:2 Leaves on the tree for "the cure of the nations" (would seem to imply corruptible bodies needing the leaves to sustain life.)

15:42-44 Incorruptible, spiritual body.

Note the Jewish Character
21:12 Twelve tribes
21:14 Twelve apostles
21:24 Nations outside city

Note the universal character
No Jewish connotations in 1 Cor 15.
In Paul's writings, no barrier between Jew and Greek.

Overall, a picture of a very physical place, with mortal Bodies...much like our present world, except with Christ reigning and keeping evil out (22:14-15)

Overall, a picture of a spiritual realm, with no corruption, no reign, no power. All are subjected. No enemies, no death, no sin, no rebellion. The purpose of the ages has been achieved. God is now All in all. How can He be All in all with death (the enemy) present?

THIS IS A DESCRIPTION OF THE FINAL AGE (EON)

THIS IS A DESCRIPTION OF THE CONSUMMATION, WHICH OCCURS AFTER THE AGES HAVE BEEN COMPLETED.

THE SAVIOUR OF ALL

The culmination of God's Word, then, is found in 1 Corinthians 15 when God becomes All in all. The book of Revelation does not take us quite this far.

With God All in all, all things have been reconciled to God, despite the plans of the enemy and the rebellion of the flesh which have seemed to triumph at times. Corruption is eliminated, and even our bodies are now incorruptible, not even needing the leaves from the tree of life to sustain life. The worst enemy of all, death, has been abolished.

In 1 Corinthians 15 we finally see every knee bowing before the Lord. The Salvation of all has not meant the ignoring of sin. The lake of fire, the second death, has accomplished its work. All men now recognize the wondrous ways of God, and His grace as expressed through the work of Christ.

The Salvation of all does not negate or minimize the work of the cross. The work of Christ upon the Cross, and the power of God as displayed through the resurrection, were both very necessary. But now, at the end of the ages, we see the true scope of God's work. Despite the sin and rebellion of humanity, God has found a way to bring every soul to the point of acceptance, and every knee now bows before Him.

The ages have ended. The purpose of the eons has now been fulfilled; to reconcile all to God. Wickedness and evil are gone. Death is no more. God is love, and He is All in all. Eternal life in perfection has begun!

STUDY & THINK FOR YOURSELF

Don't take my word for these conclusions. Do not take the word of scholars, teachers, or pastors. They do not even agree amongst themselves.

The most common teachings within the orthodox church today are based largely on traditions and teachings passed along through the church since the 5th century. These teachings are not based upon the word of God, but upon the fallible traditions of men and the fallible translations of Scripture which are confused and which are strongly influenced by the biases of the orthodox church.

In the realm of science, theories are proposed and then tested to detect error. Corrections are then made to the theory. It is the same with theology, which is simply mankind's "thoughts about God." Do not simply accept the theory (theology) that has been handed to you. Study and think for yourself!

Your current beliefs about God, and about the destiny of mankind after death, have been shaped by things you have been taught since childhood. I'm not asking you to throw out your beliefs and accept mine. I am asking you to consider what I am presenting as a theory to be tested. The old theory I was always taught, with an endless torment for the wicked, has many defects that cannot be reconciled. There were many things that appeared to be contradictions in God's Word under this old theory.

I personally see the basic theory presented in this chapter to answer many questions and eliminate many difficulties. This is not a theory I developed myself. Many have believed these things since the early days of "the church" (see the chapter titled "Testimony of Church History").

Use the methods suggested in this book to get back to the actual words used by God in the original languages. Consider the evidence. Study God's Word. Think and pray, and come to your own conclusions.

Chapter Eight

QUESTIONS ANSWERED

From the time I was a child, when I first learned that Jesus Christ was the Messiah, the Son of God, my Saviour and my Lord, I believed. Call it faith, and perhaps there was some respect for my Sunday School teachers, but I believed. And as I grew older and considered the evidence for myself, I continued to believe.

And from the time of my childhood I believed that the Bible was the Word of God. It was God revealing Himself to the world. Again, as I grew older and considered the evidence for myself, I continued to believe.

But I had questions. Learning about God in Sunday School and from the Bible was one thing. But I was forced to also consider how God was working in my life and in my world. How did these real life experiences relate to what I learned about God in Sunday School, and from the Bible?

I learned that Jesus came to this earth to die for my sins; that I might have eternal life. I learned that He was the "exact representation" of God Himself, giving us a clearer picture of God. I learned that love was the most important thing, and that God loved the world so much that He sent Jesus. I learned that love was the summary of all of God's laws and commands.

And I learned that those who accept that Jesus Christ is the Saviour in this lifetime will go to heaven when this life has ended. But those that do not accept Jesus Christ in this lifetime, regardless of how good or bad they lived their life, would go to hell where they would burn in torment and agony for eternity.

A short life, with eternal consequences, based on a single decision made while we have the chance.

"Yes, God is love, but He is also holy and requires justice," I was told. And while it did not seem to make total sense to me, if the Bible says this is how it is, then so be it.

I hungered for God's Word, and I studied the Bible and even taught adult Sunday School classes. The Bible was quite clear. There are two destinies...eternity in heaven, or eternity in hell.

I remember attending a monthly gathering of Christian businessmen in Clearwater, Florida. This was a great time of fellowship, and each month we invited a guest speaker. At one luncheon the speaker was a Messianic Jew, and in the question and answer period there were a few questions about the eternal destiny of the Jews. I'll never forget the argument that erupted; the shouting and the passion. To a faction of those present it was quite clear. Jews who did not accept Jesus Christ as the Messiah, the Saviour, in this lifetime would spend eternity in hell.

I guess I never had much of a problem with Adolph Hitler in hell, or those who commit heinous crimes. But the Jews? They were certainly faithful in seeking God in a way they thought was right. Having been raised in a Jewish family, in a Jewish school, with Jewish friends; with all of the evidence being presented to them telling them that the Messiah was still to come...it didn't seem fair that they would be in the same place as Hitler and the others.

But that's what the Bible says. It is quite simple, isn't it? It's black and white; heaven or hell; no second chance once this life is over.

I never doubted that the Bible was the Word of God. I searched the Scriptures, and kept coming up with a validation of what I had come to believe. Anyone who did not receive Jesus Christ as their

Saviour in this lifetime, regardless of how good or bad they lived, would spend eternity in hell.

I thought about people growing up in other nations, in cultures and upbringings much different from mine. I was raised in a Christian home. I was taught that Jesus Christ was the Saviour since day one. I was in Sunday School every Sunday.

I thought about young men just like me that were growing up in India. They were raised in a Hindu home. They were never taught about Jesus Christ. Maybe a missionary had reached them, but then I thought about all of the cultural pressure that told them that Jesus Christ was not the only path to salvation.

It didn't seem fair. But rules are rules. God is holy, and He cannot stand to have sin in His presence. So to get to heaven and to live in God's presence for all eternity, a person either had to live a perfect life (which no one can possibly do), or God would need to cleanse him and forgive him. God chose Jesus Christ as the means to accomplish that. So those that accept Jesus Christ as their Saviour are forgiven and will one day be given a glorified body and will live forever in heaven.

But what about my friend in India, who perhaps lived an even better life than me. Maybe he was less selfish than I. Maybe he helped other people more than I. But if he died without accepting Jesus Christ as his Saviour in this lifetime, he would stand before God on his own merits. He would be found guilty, and condemned to hell.

"God," I would plead, "isn't there a way my Indian friend can still be forgiven? Can't you still give him a glorified body fit to live in heaven? If you gave him a glorified body just like mine, wouldn't he be just as fit for heaven, to live in your presence, as I?"

I remember the Bible saying that salvation was a **gift** from God so that we who receive that gift have no right to boast. But I guess I do have some right to boast. After all, I'm smarter than my Indian friend.

I made the right decision, and he did not. My wisdom in making this decision certainly shows some intelligence on my part, doesn't it?

As I write this I am 49 years old. I remember a friend of mine who died from cancer while I was on my senior trip in high school. He was only 18. I don't know if he accepted Jesus Christ as his Saviour or not, but I think about God's justice, and I wonder why he would give me 49 years to make the right decision, and Bill only 18. But maybe since Bill suffered with cancer for several years he had time to thing about eternity, and maybe he made the right decision.

I had another friend whose brother was hit by a car and killed as he rode his bike alongside a country road. He was only 17. I guess that's old enough to make your own decisions, but when I was 17 I don't think I considered eternity all that seriously, since I thought I would have many years left. Jeff didn't have that chance.

One man lives to be 80 years old, and in his final 6 months, after living a sinful life, he accepts Jesus Christ as his Saviour. Heaven!

Another man lives to be 17 and is killed in an instant. He was told about Jesus Christ, but he did not make the right decision. Hell...forever!

"Not fair," I thought, "but this is what the Bible says." God is love, but He is also holy. To me there seemed to be a big conflict between love and justice; a big chasm. But I never doubted that the Bible was God's Word, and it is indisputable truth. Who am I to question God? I would give my friend in India a second chance after death. I would give Bill and Jeff a second chance. But the Bible made no provisions for second chances. This is the way God set things up. These were His rules, and this is His world.

As I grew older I began to lose a few aunts and uncles that I loved very much. I'm not sure where they stood with God. Some were a bit wild as far as I could detect, but I loved them, and I always thought that God loved them too!

I remember talking to some friends when I attended seminary, and we discussed what it would be like in heaven, when we find that our loved ones aren't there. One friend believed that God would kindly wipe away every memory of that loved one. I can enjoy heaven because I will have forgotten that my loved ones ever existed. This thought did not bring me great comfort. Especially now that I have five children of my own I wonder what it would be like to die, and to forget that I even had children, if they didn't make the right decision. I could better understand why some people who are not Christians have purposefully rejected Christianity, because they knew their sons and daughters and brothers and sisters made the wrong decision, and they were not intrigued by a heaven where these loved ones would not be present.

I thought again about friends my age that were dying without having accepted Jesus Christ. And I think about Saul (Paul) who was on a rampage pulling Christians right out of their homes and having them tortured and sometimes killed. But did God punish Paul? Paul had a "hardness" about him, like Osama Bin Laden. Paul condoned killing Christians and he believed he was right in doing so; even that he was serving God in doing so, like Osama Bin Laden. Paul was killing innocent people, like Osama Bin Laden. But did God give up on Paul? No! He met Him on the Road to Damascus, and struck him down, and spoke to him from the heavens, and set him straight.

Why couldn't God do that to my aunts and uncles. Why couldn't he do that with my friend in India. It didn't seem fair.

It worked out quite well for Paul. God struck him down, but he didn't kill him. It seems that it would have been awfully hard for Paul **not** to make the right decision. He was blinded and helpless. Jesus Christ actually appeared to Paul and spoke to Paul. I guess that was the only way to reach a hardened guy like Paul.

But why couldn't God do the same with everyone who needed that kind of treatment, so as to save them from spending an eternity in hell?

Sometimes my mind would wander like this, but I would always come back to the Bible. There are things that I just can't understand, but I'm not God. He created this world, and everyone in it. He can provide salvation or punishment through whatever means He chooses.

While in seminary I also came across the great preachers of old. I am told that Jonathan Edwards could really preach. He could hold his congregation spellbound. As he preached they would drop to their knees, repent, and receive Jesus Christ on the spot. In one of his sermons Mr. Edwards talked about heaven, and how the joy of those in heaven would increase even more as they looked upon those being tormented in hell. Could this be so? I guess I could somewhat understand people enjoying Hitler being tormented after the things he did, but what about Aunt Martha? There is no in-between. It's either heaven or hell. Could my joy in heaven increase as I looked upon Hitler and Aunt Martha being tormented in agony with no means to escape?

More recently I began thinking about the Garden of Eden. After all, wasn't it Adam and Eve that brought death and punishment upon us in the first place? They lived in Paradise; the perfect place. God was right there in their presence. They ate from the tree of life. There would be no death. It was perfect...or was it?

If Paradise was truly perfect, what was the serpent (Satan) doing there? He was evil, with the intent of luring Adam and Eve into sin. It doesn't seem fair. If Paradise was really Paradise it would seem that the serpent wouldn't be allowed in, and Adam and Eve wouldn't have been tempted, and perhaps they wouldn't have sinned, and maybe we wouldn't be in this mess today.

I thought this through. God placed Adam and Eve in Paradise, knowing they would be tempted, and knowing they would fall, since He had foreknown since before the disruption of the world that Christ would be a flawless and unspotted lamb. (see 1 Peter 1:20) But still He created them! And He continues to create men and women to this day, who live in a world filled with temptation, where some will accept Jesus Christ and others will not, so that He knows as He

95

creates that some of His creation is bound for the eternal torments of hell.

It doesn't really make sense, but once again I am not God, and I don't make these decisions.

I thought about all of these things, and the gulf between God's love and His justice kept getting larger (according to my reasoning), but I never doubted that the Bible was God's Word, and it was clear on the matter of heaven and hell.

But there were some Biblical issues that did seem to conflict.

The Bible says that God is the "Saviour of **all** mankind, especially of believers."

There were other "**ALL**" passages in Scripture:

>1 Corinthians 15:22 "As in Adam ***all*** are dying, thus also in Christ shall ***all*** be vivified."

>Romans 5:18 "Through one offense for ***all*** mankind for condemnation, thus also it is through one just award for ***all*** mankind for life's justifying."

>Hebrews 2:9 "He (Jesus) should be tasting death for the sake of ***everyone***."

>John 3:17 "For God does not dispatch His Son into the world that He should be judging the world, but that ***the world*** may be saved through Him."

>John 1:29 "Lo! the Lamb of God, which is taking away the sin of ***the world***."

>Colossians 1:20 "Through Him to reconcile ***all*** to Him (making peace through the blood of His cross)."

2 Corinthians 5:18 "All is of God, who conciliates us to Himself through Christ, and is giving us the dispensation of the conciliation, how that God was in Christ conciliating ***the world*** to Himself, not reckoning their offenses to them..."

Romans 11:30 "For even as you once were stubborn toward God, yet now were shown mercy at their stubbornness, thus these also are now stubborn to this mercy of yours, that now they also may be shown mercy. For God locks up all together in stubbornness, that He should be merciful to ***all***."

1 Timothy 2:6 "One Mediator of God and mankind, a Man, Christ Jesus, Who is giving Himself a correspondent Ransom for ***all***.

John 12:32 "I, if I should be exalted out of the earth, shall be drawing ***all*** to Myself."

Philippians 2:9 "***Every*** knee should be bowing...***every*** tongue should be acclaiming..." (Isaiah 45:23)

But these passages seemed to be in direct conflict with passages that talked about SOME not being saved. According to my Christian friends, it's quite simple. Since the Bible says that those who do not accept Jesus Christ in this lifetime will spend eternity in hell, these "ALL" passages must refer only to ALL who accept Christ. Now I don't see this restriction in the context of these passages, but it's the only explanation that makes God's Word consistent, instead of contradictory.

But isn't it God's will that ALL are saved?

1 Timothy 2:4 "God, who wills that ***all*** mankind be saved and come into a realization of the truth."

And doesn't He cause all things ultimately to operate in accordance with His will?

Ephesians 1:11 "...Who is operating _**all**_ in accord with the counsel of His will."

No. My Christian friends tell me that even though God "wishes" that ALL would accept Jesus Christ and be saved, He gives us free will.

So we have free will, but we're basically very fallible and weak, and to make things even more difficult we find that Satan is alive and well in this world, tempting us and leading us astray at every turn.

So even though it is God's desire that all are saved, it will not happen because He will not force anyone to make a decision against their will.

The good news is we have been given free will (although some will disagree, also with strong Biblical support). The bad news is that many will make a wrong decision in this lifetime, since they were not as smart as others so as to make the correct decision in this lifetime, and perhaps they had less time (17 years instead of 80) to make the decision, with Satan chomping at their heels at every turn.

So God will be All in all, when all is said and done (1 Corinthians 15:28), and Christ will have accomplished the purposes of God through His death and resurrection, but the bottom line is there will probably be more souls burning forever in torment than those in heaven.

These seemed like huge contradictions in Scripture, but my faith in God's Word never waivered. I may not understand the ways of God, but that doesn't mean they aren't true.

I am so thankful to have found the Concordant Version of Scripture, and the "Unsearchable Riches" magazine, published now for over 90 years. Here for the first time I learned about the many contradictions in our modern English translations which have distorted the word of God. The Word of God is perfect, as I had always thought. But I never studied deep enough to understand that there are many conflicts even between the various English translations, and the translation from the Hebrew or Greek to English is inconsistent and biased.

I began reading the back issues of "Unsearchable Riches" that showed how the Concordant Version was developed, striving for consistency and accuracy. I always liked the NIV, since it was easy to understand. I learned that it may be easy to read, but it was not too faithful to the originals.

I found in "Unsearchable Riches" how each word was meticulously studied. Sometimes there would be a ten page article focused on the translation of a single word. The best part about what I was reading was the great open-ness of this translation. Without even knowing the Hebrew or Greek, I could trace each word back to the Hebrew or Greek, and then look up every other occurrence of that Hebrew or Greek word, to see from the contexts the meaning intended.

I now see that truly the Word of God is perfect, and it is totally consistent. There are no contradictions, and also no need to impose restrictions on the "**ALL**" passages. It is only because of the errant English translations that these restrictions have arisen. It is only because of the errant English translations that there has been a great gulf between God's love and His justice. It is only because of the errant English translations that Christians argue with other Christians about things in the Bible that seem to support our various positions.

My questions have subsided. I still have some, but not as many. God **will** one day execute full justice, His holiness will prevail, death will be abolished, **every** knee will bow before Him (finally), and He will be All in all. (1 Corinthians 15) He is not willing that **any** should perish. (2 Peter 3:9) His will is that **all** will be saved, and even now He is in the process of causing all things to work in accordance with His will.

The purpose of this book is to lead you down the path I was led. I'm not asking that you believe me, but I want to show you the evidence that I have seen, so you can make your own decision.

Now things make a bit more sense!

Chapter Nine

THE TESTIMONY OF CHURCH HISTORY

Up to this point we have looked strictly at the Word of God to shape our opinions. This is as it should be! Specific information about God and His will can ***only*** be found in His revelation to mankind, and not through the speculations or thinking of mankind.

But now we turn to the history of the early church. In doing so we do not place a greater emphasis on the beliefs of the early church than upon the Word of God, but we will see that a belief in the ultimate salvation of all is not a new thing. Universalism has had its witnesses throughout the history of the church.

I am not in this chapter attempting to prove the correctness of the understandings or teachings of the "Church Fathers." When it comes to a study of the destiny of mankind, God's Word alone will be our guide. But we will see in this chapter that ***most*** average people in the first few centuries A.D., and ***many*** (if not most) of the "Church Fathers" (leaders within the church) believed in the ultimate salvation of all. Furthermore, we will see from the many direct quotations that this belief came directly from a study of God's Word.

There are many books available concerning church history, but details concerning the doctrine of Universalism are not included in the popular works. "The Ancient History of Universalism" by Hosea Ballou is strongly recommended, and is the source for many of the details provided in this chapter. Also used as sources of information for this chapter:

"The Greek Word Aion-Aionios" by Hanson
"Restitution of All Things" by Jukes
"Universal Reconciliation" by Phillips
"Christ Triumphant" by Allin
"The Modern History of Universalism" by Whittemore
"Is Hell Eternal?" by Pridgeon

Complete information on all of these works can be found in the chapter entitled "Recommended Reading." Quotes from these books include a page number for those wishing to read more.

Before observing the writings of church historians and the early "Church Fathers," we note that the term "Universalism" has nothing to do with modern universalism which has generated its views apart from the Word of God. To the early Christians, the Word of God led them to the doctrine that salvation was given to all of mankind through the death and resurrection of Jesus Christ, the Son of God.

THE SIBYLLINE ORACLES: 500 B.C. – 150 A.D.
Written by different writers between 500 B.C. and 150 A.D., the Sibylline Oracles teach eonian suffering, followed by universal salvation. If nothing else, this shows us that "eonian" was not understood as "endless" during this period.

The Sibylline books provide evidence as to the beliefs which were held in this very early time period. In one of these books the end of the world is described as a time when all things, including hades, are to be melted down in the divine fire in order to be purified. (Allin, page 109)

In the second Sibylline book, speaking of the second death in Revelation 20:14, we read that "hell" (hades) and all things and persons are cast into "unquenchable fire" for cleansing. (Allin, page 90)

THE FIRST 200 YEARS A.D.

Not many writings from this very early period are still in existence, but from the available documents we see a wide variety of beliefs concerning the future judgment and punishment.

Seven of the most prevalent "orthodox" writers from this period refer to an eternal fire or torment, but of these three obviously did not think of this "eternal" punishment as endless. Two believed in annihilation, and one believed in an ultimate restoration, despite making reference to an "eternal" punishment. The remaining four writers from the period are silent on this matter.

Ballou observes in his summary of this period in church history that there are two basic belief systems which co-existed within the church:

a. Those believing in the eventual salvation of all mankind, after a future punishment of the wicked, and
b. Those believing in eternal punishment.

What is interesting is that at this point there are no apparent divisions or controversies, despite the difference in belief as to the destiny of mankind. And we learn that to the Believers in this period, the word "eternal" does not necessarily mean endlessness, but may simply mean an indefinite period of time.

THE EARLY CREEDS

In defending eternal punishment, some will turn to the Creeds of the church. But it is interesting that for the first 500 years of Christianity not one creed hinted at eternal torment, and not one denied universal restoration, despite the fact that Universalism was very openly taught by many within the church.

Also during the first five centuries the first four General Councils were held at Nice, Constantinople, Ephesus and Chalcedon. Even though Universalism was widely and openly taught, there is no condemnation of the doctrine. No one thought it proper or necessary to include a statement concerning endless punishment in the articles of the faith.

IRENAEUS: 130 - 200 A.D.

Irenaeus viewed death as God's merciful provision for a fallen mankind. He did not believe that evil would last forever.

> "Wherefore also He drove him out of Paradise, and removed him far from the tree of life, not because He envied him the tree of life, as some dare to assert, but because He pitied him, [and desired] that he should not continue always a sinner, and that the sin which surrounded him should not be immortal, and the evil interminable and irremediable." (Jukes, page 177)

Irenaeus is credited by the historian Pfaff for the following quote:

> "Christ will come at the end of the times in order to annul everything evil, and to reconcile again all things, that there may be an end of all impurities." (Allin, page 108)

CLEMENS ALEXANDRIUS: 150 - 220 A.D.

Clemens Alexandrinus (or Clement of Alexandria), a church father who was an illustrious writer, had much to say about Universalism. The learned and orthodox Daille says, "It is manifest, throughout his works, that Clemens thought all the punishments that God inflicts upon men, are salutary, and executed by him only for the purpose of instruction and reformation." Clemens himself writes:

> "(God's) justice is, of itself, nothing but goodness; for it rewards the virtuous with blessings, and conduces to the improvement of the sinful. There are many evil affections which are to be cured only by suffering. Punishment is, in its operation, like medicine: it desolves the hard heart, purges away the filth of uncleanness, and reduces the swellings of pride and haughtiness; thus restoring its subject to a sound and

healthful state. It is not from hatred, therefore, that the Lord rebukes mankind." (Ballou, page 71)

"Wherefore, since the Lord descended to hell for no other purpose than to preach the gospel there, he preached it either to all, or only to the Jews. If to all, then all who believed there, were saved, whether Jews or Gentiles. And the chastisements of God are salutary and instructive, leading to amendment, and preferring the repentance to the death of the sinner: especially as souls in their separate state, though darkened by evil passions, have a clearer discernment than they had whilst in the body, because they are no longer clouded and encumbered by the flesh." (Ballou, page 73)

"The Lord, says he, is the propitiation, not only for our sins, that is, of the faithful, but also for the whole world (1 John 2:2): therefore he indeed saves all; but converts some by punishments, and others by gaining their free will: so that he has the high honor, that unto him every knee should bow, of things in heaven, on earth, and under the earth..." (Ballou, page 74)

"We can set no limits on the agency of the Redeemer: to redeem, to rescue, to discipline, in his work, and so will he continue to operate after this life." (Quoted from Neander in Hanson, page 118)

"All men are Christ's, some by knowing Him, the rest not yet. He is the Saviour, not of some (only) and of the rest not...for how is He Lord and Saviour if He is not Lord and Saviour of all?...But He is indeed Saviour of those who believe...while of those who do not believe He is Lord, until having become able to confess Him, they obtain through Him the benefit appropriate and suitable (to their case)...He by the Father's will directs the salvation of all." (Allin, page 107)

"But needful correction, by the goodness of the great overseeing Judge, through (by means of) the attendant angels, through various prior judgments, through the final (pantelous) judgment, compels even those who have become still more callous to repent." (Allin, page 107)

"So Christ saves all men. Some He converts by penalties, others who follow Him of their own will…that every knee may be bent to Him, of those in heaven, on earth, and under the earth." (Allin, page 108)

"Therefore He indeed saves all universally; but some as converted by punishments, others by voluntary submission." (Jukes, page 176)

"He punishes for their good those who are punished, whether collectively or individually." (Jukes, page 184)

"For all things are arranged with a view to the salvation of the universe by the Lord of the universe both generally and particularly."

Like all the early church fathers, Clemens held to a position of free will, but he believes in the power of God to lead all mankind, through a variety of means, to an ultimate subjection to Him.

THEOPHILUS: 169 – 181 A.D.

Theophilus, Bishop of Antioch, wrote in "To Autolycus" (Book 2, Chapter 26):

"And God showed great kindness to man in this, that He did not suffer him to continue being in sin forever; but, as it were by a kind of banishment, cast him out of Paradise, in order that, having by punishment expiated within an appointed time the sin, and having been disciplined, he should afterward be recalled." (Pridgeon, page 281)

ORIGEN: 185 - 254 A.D.

Origen Adamantius was respected in his lifetime as few others have ever been. He was the most learned man of his day, and many examples from his writings show that "aionian" did not mean "endless" during the time that he wrote.

In roughly 230 A.D. he published "Of Principles" in which he advocated, at length, universal salvation. Throughout his lifetime, Universalism was a favorite topic for Origen. Following are a few direct quotes:

"The end and consummation of the world will take place, when all shall be subjected to punishments proportioned to their several sins; and how long each one shall suffer, in order to receive his deserts, God only knows. But we suppose that the goodness of God, through Christ, will certainly restore all creatures into one final state; his very enemies being overcome and subdued." (Ballou, page 87)

"The apostle Paul says that Christ must reign till he hath put all enemies under his feet. But if there is any doubt what is meant by putting enemies under his feet, let us hear the apostle still further, who says, for ALL things must be subjected to him (1 Corinthians 15)...For the very expression, *subjected to Christ*, denotes the salvation of those who are subjected." (Ballou, page 87)

"Such, then, being the final result of things, that all enemies shall be subdued to Christ, death the last enemy be destroyed, and the kingdom be delivered up to the Father, by Christ." (Ballou, page 87)

"The sacred scripture does, indeed, call our God a consuming fire (Deuteronomy 4:24), and says that rivers of fire go before his face (Daniel 7:10), and that he shall come as a refiner's fire and as fuller's soap, and purify the people (Malachi 3:2). As, therefore, God is a consuming fire, what is it that is to be consumed by him? We say it is wickedness, and whatever proceeds from it, such as is figuratively called wood, hay and stubble." (Ballou, page 112)

"But he who shall have spurned the cleansing which is effected by the Gospel of God, will reserve himself for a dreadful and penal course of purification; for the fire of hell shall, by its torments, purify him whom neither the apostolic doctrine, nor the evangelical word has cleansed; as it is written, *I will thoroughly purify you with fire.* (Isaiah 1:25) But how long, or for how many ages, sinners shall be tormented in this course of purification which is effected by the pain of fire, he only knows to whom the Father hath committed all judgment, and who so loved his creatures that for them he laid aside the form of God, took the form of a servant, and humbled himself unto death, that all men might be saved and come to the knowledge of the truth."
(Ballou, page 118)

"When the Son is said to be subject to the Father, the perfect restoration of the whole creation is signified." (Allin, page 110)

Origen has been described by many historians as a most qualified scholar, well versed in the Holy Scriptures. Of Origen the historian Phillip Schaff writes:

"It is impossible to deny a respectful sympathy to this extraordinary man, who with all his brilliant talents, and a host of enthusiastic friends and admirers, was driven from his country, stripped of his sacred office, excommunicated from part of the church, then thrown into a dungeon, lead with chains, racked by torture, doomed to drag his aged frame and dislocated limbs in pain and poverty, and long after his death to have his memory branded, his name anathematized and his salvation denied; but who nevertheless did more than all his enemies combined to advance the cause of sacred learning, to refute and convert heathens and heretics, and to make the church respected in the eyes of the world."

In his "A History of Christ," Latourette writes of Origen:

> "Origen was more than a great teacher: He was on fire with the Christian faith."

> "His was, indeed, one of the greatest Christian minds."

> "A superb teacher, he had a profound influence upon his students. From them and through his writing issued currents which were to help mold Christian thought for generations."

In his "History of the Christian Church," Phillip Schaff writes:

> "Origen is one of the most important witnesses of the anteNicene text of the Greek Testament, which is older than the received text...The value of his testimony is due to his rare opportunities and life-long study of the Bible before the time when the traditional Syrian and Byzantine text was formed. Origen was an uncommonly prolific author, but by no means an idle bookmaker. Jerome says he wrote more than other men can read. Epiphanius, an opponent of Origen, states the number of his works as six thousand, which is perhaps not much beyond the mark."

Now we look at the words of Origen as he debates with a Greek philosopher named Celsus:

> "The Stoics, indeed, hold that, when the strongest of the elements prevails, all things shall be turned into fire. But our belief is that the Word shall prevail over the entire rational creation, and change every soul into his own perfection...for although in the diseases and wounds of the body, there are some which no medical skill can cure, yet we hold that in the mind there is no evil so strong that it may not be overcome by the Supreme Word and God. For stronger than all the evils in the soul is the Word, and the healing power that swells in

Him, and the healing He applies, according to the will of God to every man."

"The consummation of all things is the destruction of evil...to quote Zephaniah: 'My determination is to gather the nations, that I may assemble the kings, to pour upon them mine indignation, even all my fierce anger, for all the earth shall be devoured with the fire of my jealousy. For then will I turn to the people a pure language, that they may call upon the Lord, to serve Him with one consent.' Consider carefully the promise, that all shall call upon the name of the Lord and serve Him with one consent; also that all contemptuous reproach shall be taken away, and there shall be no longer any injustice or vain speech, or a deceitful tongue." (Celsus 6k8, ch 72, ANJ w4, p667)

Origen provides some valuable evidence as to the use of the word "everlasting" during this era. While Origen refers to sufferings as "everlasting," he holds that they are actually of as short or long a period of time as God deems appropriate or necessary. In his works he often uses the expressions "everlasting fire" or "everlasting punishment," while the quotations we have already seen clearly show that to Origen these things are not endless in terms of time.

Interestingly, Theodore of Mopsuestia, an opponent of Origen, agreed with him in calling the future penalty "eternal," when he actually taught that it would be in all cases temporary. (Allin, page 90)

In Origen's writings he never treats Universalism as a topic which is counter to orthodox teachings. It is interesting that despite Origen's voluminous writings, no one seems to take issue with his Universalism during his lifetime. Origen was challenged by the church in his day, but not concerning his views on Universalism. About forty years after Origen's death, controversy arose over his writings, but again no attack was made upon his stance on universal salvation, until the contention lasted a century.

Origen's influence was far stronger in the Eastern (Greek) churches than in the West (Latin), probably due at least in part to the language difference.

GREGORY THAUMATURGUS: 220 - 250 A.D.

Gregory Thaumaturgus, a student of Origen, became one of the most eminent bishops of the time. It was well known that Gregory held to the doctrine of Universal Restoration.

AFTER ORIGEN'S DEATH: 254 TO 390 A.D.

During this time period no evidence is found to imply that Origen's Universalism created any controversy within the church, even though his writings were scrutinized and were often attacked in other subject matters. Even Epiphanius, bishop of Salamis (Cyprus), a believer in endless punishment, did not attack Origen's doctrine of Universalism, even though he persecuted the "Origenists" (followers of Origen) around 376 A.D.

Between 370 and 383 A.D. Universalism seems to have been, at least for a time, the belief of a ***majority*** of the most eminent orthodox church fathers in the East. Gregory Nyssen, Didymus, and Jerome advocated Universalism, while Gregory Nazianzen vacillated between this doctrine and the doctrine of endless punishment. The latter wrote:

> "Adam receives death as a gain, and thereby the cutting off of sin; that evil should not be immortal: and so the penalty turns out a kindness, for thus I am of opinion it is God punishes." (Pridgeon, page 284)

In this era it appears that the majority of early Christians believed that all mankind, through Christ, would be ultimately restored. St. Basil the Great (c. 329-379) was not a believer in the doctrine of universal reconciliation, but he writes in his "De Asceticis,"

> "The mass of men (Christians) say that there is to be an end of punishment to those who are punished." (Allin, page 149)

A momentous event in church history took place in 313 A.D. when Christianity was officially declared tolerable. In the years that followed, Christianity continued to grow in favor with Constantine. But as persecution gave way to acceptance, councils frequently assembled, and arguments ensued. Deposition and excommunication were decreed. But even in the midst of this, Athanasius, the guardian of the Nicene faith, always quoted Origen as orthodox.

Lest we think of the church leaders of this age as without blemish, the highly respected Gregory Nazianzen described the clergy as "avaricious, quarrelsome, licentious, and unprincipled." Gregory said of the frequent councils which were called during this era that he was afraid of them, because he had never seen the end of one that was happy and pleasant. (Ballou, page 181)

NOTES FROM CHURCH HISTORIANS

Ethelbert Stauffer, writing on the early church:
> "The primitive church never gave up the hope that in His will to save, the All-Merciful and All-Powerful God would overcome even the final 'no' of the self-sufficient world." (Phillips, page 44)

According to historian Henry Nutcomb Oxenham:
> "The doctrine of endless punishment was not believed at all by some of the holiest and wisest of the Fathers, and was not taught as an integral part of the Christian faith by any even of those who believed it as an opinion."

The historian Pfaff writes:
> "The ultimate restoration of the lost was an opinion held by very many Jewish teachers, and some of the Fathers." (Allin, page 80)

Dietelmaier reports:

> "Universalism in the fourth century drove its roots down deeply, alike in the East and West, and had very many defenders." (Allin, page 80)

Reuss reports:

> "The doctrine of a general restoration of all rational creatures has been recommended by very many of the greatest thinkers of the ancient church, and of modern times." (Allin, page 80)

C. B. Schleuter:

> "Indeed, beside Origen, Gregory of Nyssa also, Gregory of Nazianzus, Basil, Ambrose himself, and Jerome, taught everywhere the universal restitution of things, asserting simultaneously with it, an end of eternal punishment." (Allin, page 80)

In the Schaff-Herzog "The Encyclopedia of Religious Knowledge" (1908) we read in volume 12, page 96:

> "In the first five or six centuries of Christianity there were six theological schools, of which four (Alexandria, Antioch, Caesarea, and Edessa or Nisibis) were Universalist; one (Ephesus) accepted conditional immortality; one (Carthage or Rome) taught endless punishment of the wicked."

Geisler, a great church historian, writes:

> "The opinion of the indestructible capacity for reformation in all rational creatures, and the finiteness of the torments of hell, was so common in the West, and so widely diffused among opponents of Origen, that though it might not have sprung up without the influence of his school, yet it had become quite independent of it." (Eccles Hist 1-212 and Pridgeon, page 283)

> "The Eastern Church of that time (fourth and fifth centuries) was permeated, from Gregory of Nyssa downwards, with the wider Hope." (Allin, page 127)

EUSEBIUS OF CAESAREA: 265 – 340 A.D.

Eusebius, Bishop of Caesarea in Palestine and friend of Constantine, wrote:

> "The Son 'breaking in pieces' His enemies is for the sake of remolding them, as a potter his own work, as Jeremiah 18:6 says: i.e., to restore them once again to their former state." (Phillips, page 42 and Allin, page 112)

> "Christ, caring for the salvation of all…and bursting the eternal gates, opened a way of return to life for the dead bound in chains of death." (Allin, page 99)

> "Christ will descend in order that all, both on earth and in heaven and in hades, may obtain salvation from Him." (Allin, page 98)

ATHANASIUS: 296 – 373 A.D.

Especially known for defending the deity of Christ, Athanasius, Bishop of Alexandria, was called "Father of Orthodoxy." He writes:

> "While the devil thought to kill one he is deprived of all…cast out of hades, and sitting by the gates, sees all the fettered beings led forth by the courage of the Saviour." (Allin, page 99)

MARCELLUS OF ANCYRA: 315 A.D.

Some of the writings of Marcellus were preserved by Eusebius:

> "For what else do the words mean, 'Until the times of restitution' (Acts 3:21) but that the Apostle designed to point out that time, in which all things partake of that perfect restoration." (Allin, page 112)

DIDYMUS – ROUGHLY 300 TO 390 A.D.

Didymus "the blind" of Alexandria was one of the most learned men of this time period. Blind at the age of five, he made himself a master of grammar, rhetoric, logic, music, arithmetic and mathematics. He was elected President of the great Catechetical School in Alexandria. Jerome said that Didymus surpassed all of his day in knowledge of the Scriptures.

Jerome also said that Didymus was "a most avowed advocate of Origen." (Allin, page 125) From his writings and from the fact that he was condemned for his views over 150 years later by the General Council of Constantinople, we know that Didymus was clearly a Universalist.

"A Dictionary of the Bible" by Hastings reports:

> "Didymus was a zealous Universalist who explicitly endorsed Origen's opinion on the conversion of devils."

Didymus himself writes:

> "Mankind, being reclaimed from their sins…are to be subjected to Christ in the fullness of the dispensation instituted for the salvation of all." (Commentary on 1 Peter 3)

Didymus was a voluminous writer, but only a few of his works survived the passing of time and the destruction by decree of later councils. During his lifetime he was fully accepted as orthodox.

GREGORY NYSSEN: 332 - 398 A.D.

A respected bishop and theologian who followed many of Origen's teachings, Gregory Nyssen (or Gregory of Nyssa) taught frequently on the matter of Universalism, and it could even be said that Universalism was at the very heart of his teachings. Yet Gregory was always well respected, and considered to be very orthodox. Following are a few direct quotations:

"The nature of evil shall, at length, be wholly exterminated, and divine, immortal goodness embrace within itself every rational creature; so that of all who were made by God, not one shall be excluded from his kingdom. All the viciousness, that like a corrupt matter is mingled in things, shall be dissolved and consumed in the furnace of purgatorial fire; and everything that had its origin from God, shall be restored to its pristine state of purity." (Ballou, page 188)

[Speaking on 1 Corinthians 15:22-28] "It is manifest that here the apostle declares the extinction of all sin, saying, that God will be all in all. For God will be truly all in all only when no evil shall remain in the nature of things, as he is never engaged in evil..." (Ballou, page 189)

"Whoever considers the divine power will plainly perceive that it is able at length to restore by means of the everlasting purgation and expiatory sufferings, those who have gone even to this extremity of wickedness." (Hanson, page 73)

"Therefore the Divine judgment does not as its chief object cause pain to those who have sinned, but works good alone by separating from evil, and drawing to a share in blessedness." (Pridgeon, page 286)

"If this (sin) be not cured here, its cure is postponed to a future life." (Pridgeon, page 286)

"(The judgment) is believed to be a medicine, a cure from God, who is bringing the creature, which he has formed, back to that state of grace which first existed." (Pridgeon, page 286)

"For it is needful that evil should some day be wholly and absolutely removed out of the circle of being." (Jukes, page 179)

"Our Lord is the One who delivers man (all men), and who heals the inventor of evil himself." (Phillips, page 42)

Like others of his day, Gregory often used the word "everlasting" when speaking of future punishment, but clearly affixed a different meaning to the word than we do today.

Gregory was always viewed as one of the most influential leaders of orthodoxy, and he was not condemned for his very blatant views concerning Universalism during his lifetime. The historian Neander writes:

> "But this particular doctrine (of the final restitution of all) was expounded and maintained with the greatest ability in works written expressly for that purpose by Gregory of Nyssa...All punishments are means of purification, ordained by divine love to purge rational beings from moral evil, and to restore them back to that communion with God which corresponds to their nature. God would not have permitted the existence of evil, unless He had forseen that by the Redemption all rational beings would in the end, according to their destination, attain to the same blessed fellowship with Himself." (Pridgeon, page 287)

It was not until two or three centuries after his death that Gregory's Universalism became a point of contention.

HILLARY: 354 A.D.

Hillary, Bishop of Poictiers, is considered one of the champions of orthodoxy. He very much respected the writings of Origen, and translated some 40,000 lines of Origen's writings according to Jerome. Hillary said:

> "The whole human race, who are one, are the one lost sheep, which is destined to be found by the Good Shepherd." (Allin, page 114)

As for giving Christ the ends of the earth as His possession, Hillary insists this refers to a universal dominion which is summed up

117

in Paul's words, "That every knee of things in heaven, and earth, and under the earth, are to bend in Jesus' name." (Allin, page 114)

EVAGRIUS PONTICUS: ROUGHLY 390 A.D.

Evagrius Ponticus was a respected scholar and monk, and a Universalist. Due to the later condemnation of Universalism over 150 years after his death, most of his writings were destroyed.

AMBROSE OF MILAN: 339 TO 397 A.D.

Most of the others mentioned were from the Eastern church, but now we turn to the Western church to look at Ambrose, archbishop of Milan in Italy. Ambrose was a man of moderate learning, but he became a very powerful figure in the church, and in the state.

Ambrose believed that nearly all who are tried on Judgment Day would sooner or later be saved. He did speak of a class of individuals, the impious or infidels, who, along with the Devil and his angels, would have no chance for restoration.

> "As for those who do not come to the first, but are reserved until the second resurrection, these shall be burnt, until they fulfill their appointed times, between the first and the second resurrection; or, if they should not have fulfilled them then, they shall remain still longer in punishment." (Jukes, page 186)

> "The Lord descends to the infernal world, in order that even those, who were in the infernal abodes, should be set free from their perpetual bonds." (Allin, page 100)

> Christ, when among the dead, "gave pardon to those in the infernal abodes, destroying the law of death." (Allin, page 100)

> "What, then, hinders our believing that he who is beaten small as the dust is not annihilated, but is changed for the better; so

that, instead of an earthly man, he is made a spiritual man, and our believing that he who is destroyed, is so destroyed that all taint is removed, and there remains but what is pure and clean." (Allin, page 130)

"God gave death, not as a penalty, but as a remedy...death was given for a remedy as the end of evil...God did not appoint death from the beginning, but gave it as a remedy." (Allin, page 130)

"The mystery of the Incarnation is the salvation of the entire creation...as it is elsewhere said, 'the whole creation shall be set free from the bondage of corruption." (Allin, page 131)

"So the Son of Man came to save that which was lost, i.e., all, for as in Adam all die, so, too, in Christ shall all be made alive." (Allin, page 132)

Ambrose insisted that subjection to Christ is loving submission, and that in this sense *all* must become Christ's subjects.

"Christ will be subject to God in us by means of the obedience of all...when vices having been cast away, and sin reduced to submission, one spirit of all people, in one sentiment, shall with one accord begin to cleave to God, then God will be All in All." (Allin, page 131)

THE FIRST CENSURE AGAINST UNIVERSALISM: 394 A.D.

It was not until 394 A.D. that we find the first censure, on record, of Universalism. But at this point the censure is not against the salvation of all mankind, but opposes only the salvation of the devil.

ORIGEN STILL RESPECTED IN 397 – 398 A.D.

Origen's books "Of Principles" were still readily accepted by many in Rome, and his teachings were accepted by a number of priests, monks and common Christians. Around this time, though, some opposition arose and Marcella, a lady of influence, succeeded in rousing a fury. Still, it seems during this time that even Jerome's circle did not consider "Of Principles" to be heretical.

JEROME: 340 – 420 A.D.

Jerome began by supporting the view of a restoration from hell.

> "The nations are gathered to the Judgment, that on them may be poured out all the wrath of the fury of the Lord, and this in pity and with a design to heal…in order that every one may return to the confession of the Lord, that in Jesus' Name every knee may bow, and every tongue may confess that He is Lord. All God's enemies shall perish, not that they cease to exist, but cease to be enemies…" (Phillips, page 43)

> "What I mean is, the fallen angel will begin to be that which he was created, and man, who has been expelled from Paradise, will be once more restored to the tilling of Paradise. These things, then, will take place universally." (Allin, page 134)

> "With God, no rational creature perishes eternally." (Allin, page 134)

> "Death shall come as a visitor to the impious; it will not be perpetual; it will not annihilate them; but will prolong its visit, till the impiety which is in them shall be consumed." (Allin, page 134)

In one instance Jerome referred to the fire of Gehenna as "purifying." (Allin, page 92)

Jerome had actually incorporated some of the writings of Origen and others into his own works, without censuring the writings in any way. Under growing pressure, Jerome changed his position and began to deny the salvation of the devil and of the damned. But even with

120

his new position, he did not appear to consider Universalism one of the significant errors of Origen.

Even while distancing himself from the writings of Origen, Jerome still continued to quote Origen as a qualified expounder of scripture. Later in life, though, he kept silent on the issue of Universalism. But as to the prevalence of the doctrine of Universalism in his day, Jerome states:

> "I know that most persons understand by the story of Ninevah and its king, the ultimate forgiveness of the devil and all rational creatures." (Allin, page 150)

Jerome once went so far as to say in a letter that Origen was condemned not on account of his doctrines, but because of jealousy. (Allin, page 135)

TITUS: 340 – 370 A.D.

Titus, bishop of Bostra, was referred to by Jerome as "one of the most important church writers of his time." Titus wrote:

> The "abyss of hell is, indeed, the place of torment; but it is not eternal, nor did it exist in the original constitution of nature. It was made afterwards, as a remedy for sinners, that it might cure them. And the punishments are holy, as they are remedial and salutary in their effect upon transgressors; for they are inflicted, not to preserve them in their wickedness, but to make them cease from their wickedness." (Ballou, page 169)

JOHN CASSIAN: 360 – 435 A.D.

John Cassian is described in the Schaff-Herzog Encyclopedia as follows:

> "Under the instruction of these great teachers (Theodore of Mopsuestia and John Cassian) many theologians believed in

universal salvation; and indeed the whole Eastern Church until after 500 A.D. was inclined to it."

DIODORE: 370 – 390 A.D.

Diodore was bishop of Tarsus and bishop of Jerusalem. In McClintock-Strong's "Cyclopedia of Biblical Theological and Ecclesiastical Literature," Diodore is described as:

"A teacher of great repute in the school of Antioch, and afterwards bishop of Jerusalem, was also a Universalist, who, in opposition to the then general prevalence of allegorical interpretation, strictly adhered to the natural import of the text in his many commentaries on the Scriptures.

He defended Universalism on the ground that the divine mercy far exceeds all the effects and all the deserts of sin."

Diodore himself wrote:

"For the wicked are punished, not perpetual, but they are to be tormented for a certain brief period…according to the amount of malice in their works. They shall therefore suffer punishment for a short space, but immortal blessedness, having no end awaits them…the penalties to be inflicted for their many and grave crimes are very far surpassed by the magnitude of the mercy to be shewed them. The resurrection, therefore is regarded as a blessing not only to the good but also to the evil." (Allin, page 137)

GREGORY OF NAZIANZUS: 370 A.D.

President of the second great Ecumenical Council, Gregory of Nazianzus was considered the most learned bishop in one of the most learned ages of the Church. (Allin, page 117)

Perhaps the foremost man in the entire Church during his day, Gregory raised no objection to the teaching of Universalism, and there is reason to contend that he himself held this belief. He taught that when Christ descended into hades, He liberated all the souls there in prison, not just some of them. (Allin, page 118)

RUFINUS: 390 A.D.

Rufinus clearly taught that the future punishment of the wicked was to be temporary. (Allin, page 137)

THEODORET THE BLESSED: 393 – 466 A.D.

Theodoret the Blessed was bishop of Cyrrhus, or Cyprus, in Syria, and a historian. He continued the historian Eusibius' work to 428 A.D. McClintock-Strong describes Theodoret as, "a pupil of Theodore of Mopsuestia, was also a Universalist holding the doctrine on the theory advocated by the Antiochian school."

Theodoret writes:

> "He shews the reason of penalty, for the Lord, who loves men, chastises in order to heal, like a physician, that he may arrest the course of our sin." (Hom in Ezech., ch 6; and in Jukes, page 184-5)

> As all men became mortal through Adam, "so shall the whole nature of mankind (all men) follow the Lord Christ, and be made partaker of the Resurrection." (Allin, page 144)

> "For the Lord, the lover of men, torments us only to cure us, that He may put a stop to the course of our iniquity." (Pridgeon, page 288)

Theodoret describes Christ as saying to the devil:

> "I mean to open the prison of death for the rest, but will shut up thee only." (Allin, page 102)

Theodoret clearly teaches that death is a medicine, not a penalty. According to Theodoret, to imagine that God, in anger at a little eating, inflicted death as a penalty, is to copy the abominable (heretic) Marcion. (Allin, page 140)

PERSECUTION OF "THE ORIGENISTS"

As opposition grew, some of the Origenists fell under great persecution, including a group of Origenist monks at Nitria who were captured and tortured.

Theophilus called a Synod of bishops at Alexandria in 399 A.D. and a decree was issued condemning Origen, and athematizing all who approved of his works. This was the first decree of its kind. Origenists fled to other countries.

Anastasius, the new Pope in 400 A.D. issued a decree which was received through all the West, condemning the works of Origen.

UNIVERSALISM STILL NOT CONDEMNED

What is most amazing is that now, nearly 400 years after the departure of Christ, we see the very first official condemnations of Origen, but even now his view on the salvation of all mankind has not been condemned. The salvation of the devil and his angels is here condemned along with some other issues, but the salvation of all mankind is not addressed. As a matter of fact, during this time period some of the orthodox clearly continue to hold to this doctrine.

Others who deserve mention from this time period who supported the doctrine of Universalism are the Basilidians (130 A.D.), the Carpocratians (140 A.D.), Isidore of Alexandria (370-400 A.D.) and Palladius of Gallatia (400 A.D.).

AUGUSTINE: 354 - 430 A.D.

When a disturbance over various theological issues arose at Tarraco (Spain), two of the bishops called upon Augustine in Africa.

Augustine immediately wrote a small book, "Against the Priscillianists and Origenists," opposing Universalism and asserting eternal punishment. In this book Augustine maintained that the original word translated "everlasting" *always* meant "endless," but later he was forced to abandon this stance, claiming that the word only sometimes meant "endless."

Admitting that there might be some exceptions, he used Matthew 25:46 as his overriding authority, where the same Greek word is used for the torments of the damned as for the life of the saints. Augustine reasoned that if "eternal punishment" was limited in duration, so also must "eternal life."

It appears that this is the very earliest claim that the original word "aionian" must mean "endless." It is interesting to note that Augustine was a Latin writer, and very imperfectly aquainted with Greek!

Augustine's opinions carried great weight within the church, especially in the West. Because of his influence, and because of the ignorance of both Greek and Hebrew for most men in the years to follow, the doctrine of universal reconciliation became silenced until its revival in the 16th century, and the doctrine of an endless torment became the norm within the orthodox church.

By all accounts, Augustine was a great man. He was very familiar with the scriptures, competent in his learning, warm, devotional, pious, moral, and very fair even with his opponents. He became the father of the present orthodox system. But Augustine was, like many of the other church fathers, a hasty writer, and not strong in the Greek language.

As a final note on Augustine; while he was one of the strongest proponents of the doctrine of eternal torment, he admits:

> "There are very many who though not denying the Holy Scriptures, do not believe in endless torments." (Enchiria, ad Laurent, c. 29 and Allin, page 150)

It is interesting that in making this observation, Augustine does not declare those not believing in endless torments to be unorthodox.

INFLUENCE OF THE LATIN VULGATE TRANSLATION

It would seem that the more learned a Christian was in the original languages, the more likely he or she was to see the doctrine of the restitution of all things. Augustine, who said he hated the Greek language and who read only the Latin Vulgate translation, began to incline toward the doctrine of eternal torment. The Greek "aion" which meant "age" was translated into the Latin Vulgate as "aeternum" (eternal) and "seculum." This continues to corrupt our English translations even today. The Latin church separated themselves from the original languages and began to teach what the pagan religions had taught for centuries...eternal torment.

CYRIL OF ALEXANDRIA: 412 A.D.

Cyril frequently taught that every soul would be freed from hades by Christ.

> "The devil was deprived of all power of being able to do anything for the future...The souls of men who had been caught in his toils to their ruin, came out of the underground gates, and, leaving the hiding places of the pit, escape." (Allin, page 143)

Cyril describes that Christ spoiled hades, and:

> "left the devil there solitary and deserted." (Allin, page 102)

THEODORUS: 380 TO 429 A.D.

Theodorus (or Theodore), bishop of Mopsuestia, was an eminent orthodox father in the Eastern church, and a voluminous writer. He was not a follower of Origen, and even opposed his allegorical system of interpreting scripture. But he was clearly a believer in Universalism.

Theodore, and perhaps Diodorus, after they were dead for 125 years, were condemned as Nestorians in the Fifth Council, a gathering that was unrecognized by many. But even here their position favoring Universalism was not raised as an issue.

Some quotations from Theodore:

> "All have the hope of rising with Christ, so that the body having obtained immortality, thenceforeward the proclivity to evil should be removed." (Allin, page 142)

> God "recapitulated all things in Christ...as though making a compendious renewal, and restoration of the whole creation, through Him,...Now this will take place in a future age, when all mankind and all powers (virtues) possessed of reason, look up to Him, as is right, and obtain mutual concord and firm peace." (Allin, page 143)

MAXIMUS OF TURIN: 422 A.D.

Maximus appears from his extant writings to teach the liberation of all souls from hades, and that the purpose of death is to correct the sinner.

> "He must of necessity have destroyed the sins of all, Who bore the sins of all, as says the Evangelist: 'The Lamb of God Who taketh away the sins of the world.'...We read in the Scriptures, that the salvation of the entire human race, was won by the Redemption of the Saviour...the everlasting safety of the entire world." (Allin, page 144)

430 TO 450 A.D.

Universalism was accepted by a significant number of monks around Cesarea in Palestine.

PETER CHRYSOLOGUS: 435 A.D.
Peter Chrysologus, bishop of Ravenna, said in a sermon on the Good Shepherd that the lost sheep represents:

> "...the whole human race lost in Adam," and that Christ "followed the one, seeks the one in order that in the one he may restore all." (Allin, page 140)

GENNADIUS: 458 A.D.
Gennadius, Patriarch of Constantinople, said:

> "The firstfruits shall obtain the totality and the rest of the body shall follow the head...For, said He, when lifted up, I will draw all men unto Myself." (Allin, page 152)

BARSUDAILI (HIEROTHEUS): END OF 5TH CENTURY
Toward the end of the fifth century Barsudaili, an Abbot of Edessa, taught Universalism under the name "Hierotheus." He asserted the eventual end of all penalties, and their purifying character. Even the fallen spirits are to receive mercy, and all things are to be restored, so that God may be All in all. (Allin, page 154)

JUSTINIAN: 540 A.D.
Justinian ruled the throne of the eastern empire, and was one of the few sovereigns who had ambitions of taking part in theological disputes. He ordered a long Edict to be drawn up, addressed to Mennas (archbishop of Constantinople), which was published around 540 A.D. This decree was aimed directly against Universalism, and went forth with the full force of law in the land.

ALEXANDER OF ABYLA: 540 TO 546 A.D.

Alexander, bishop of Abyla, was bold enough to stand against the emperor's authority. As a result he was excluded from the catholic communion.

THE HOME SYNOD: 541 A.D.

In 541 A.D. the Emperor Justinian caused the Patriarch Mennas to convene at Constantinople the "Home Synod," for the purpose of condemning Universalism and other teachings of Origen. The Synod passed fifteen Canons condemning various teachings of Origen, but they deliberately omitted any condemnation of Universalism. (Allin, page 162)

THE FIFTH GENERAL COUNCIL: 553 A.D.

Under the watchful eye of Emperor Justinian, the Fifth General Council was opened in Constantinople with 151 bishops present from the Greek and African churches. During the course of the meeting, Justinian sent a message exhorting the bishops to examine the doctrine of "the impious Origen," and to condemn him and his followers.

Included in the actions of the council:

"Whoever says or thinks that the torments of the demons and of impious men are temporal, so that they will, at length, come to an end, or whoever holds a restoration either of the demons or of the impious, let him be anathema."

This decree fixed the orthodox faith to the present day.

MAXIMUS: 645 A.D.

Maximus criticized the teachings of Gregory of Nyssa, but he did teach Universalism.

"For it is necessary that as all nature is to receive at the Resurrection immortality of the flesh...so, too, the fallen powers of the soul must, in the process of the ages, cast off the memories of sin implanted in them, and having passed all the ages...come to God; and so by the knowledge, not the fruition of good, receive strength and be restored to their original state." (Allin, page 155)

CLEMENT OF IRELAND: 740 A.D.

Clement, a native of Ireland, became an ordained minister in the Romish communion. He later discarded certain superstitions of the church, renounced its authority, rejected its decrees, and insisted that the Bible _only_ was to be the authoritative guide to faith. He taught that Christ, when he descended into hell, restored all the damned.

Clement gathered several independent congregations in France and Germany.

In 744 A.D. Clement was deposed from the priesthood, condemned as a heretic, and imprisoned. It is probable that he died in prison.

JOHN PICUS: 1480 TO 1494

John Picus, earl of Mirandola and Concordia, was a distinguished scholar in Italy. He alarmed the church during this period by advancing his theological opinions.

"Infinite pain is not due even to mortal sin; because sin is finite, and therefore merits but finite punishment." (Ballou, page 320)

The Pope ordered his examination, and brought a judgment censuring Picus, forbidding the reading of his books.

MARTIN LUTHER: 1483 - 1546

The reader may be surprised to find that the following words are attributed to the well known reformer, Martin Luther:

> "God forbid that I should limit the time of acquiring faith to the present life. In the depth of the Divine mercy there may be opportunity to win it in the future." (Phillips, page 43)

DANIEL DEFOE: 1660 - 1731

Daniel DeFoe, author of "Robinson Crusoe" was throughout his life an "orthodox nonconformist." His belief in the ultimate reconciliation of all is expressed in an interchange between Crusoe and Friday concerning the Devil, when Friday concludes, "So you, I, Devil, all wicked, all preserve, repent, God pardon all."

WILLIAM LAW: 1686 - 1761

William Law, author of the classic "A Serious Call to a Devout and Holy Life," came to his belief in universal reconciliation in the latter part of his life. Law writes:

> "that all the attributes of the Almighty are only modifications of his love, and that when, in Scripture his wrath, vengeance, etc. are spoken of, such expressions are only used in condescension to human weakness, by way of adapting the subject of the mysterious workings of God's providence to human capacities."

Law held that God punishes no one, and that all evil originates either from matter, from the free will of man, and God permits suffering for the sake of a greater good. All beings will finally be happy. (From Southey's "Life of Wesley" as reported in Whittemore, page 188.)

GEORGE STONEHOUSE: 1714 - 1793

Sir George Stonehouse, a staunch Universalist, was a member of the well known "Holy Club" led by John and Charles Wesley, and which also included George Whitfield. Between 1729 and 1735 the doctrine of Universalism was debated with great interest by the club. What is most interesting is that Stonehouse was never expelled from the group, and Wesley never found it necessary to officially address the arguments raised publicly by Stonehouse.

THOMAS NEWTON: 1761

Thomas Newton was nominated Bishop of Bristol in 1761, and was well respected as a man of learning and virtue. Newton wrote:

> "God is love, and he would rather not have given life, than render that life a torment and curse to all eternity...His chastisements, like those of a loving father, are designed, not to harden men in sin, but to recover them to goodness, to correct and meliorate their nature."

> "Imagine a creature, nay imagine numberless creatures, produced out of nothing, and therefore guilty of no prior offence, sent into this world of frailty, which it is well known beforehand they will so use as to abuse it, and then for the excesses of a few years delivered over to torments of endless ages, without the least hope or possibility of relaxation or redemption. Imagine it you may, but you can never seriously believe it, nor reconcile it to God and goodness." (Whittemore, page 233)

JOHN HENDERSON: 1757 - 1788

John Henderson was born in Ireland in 1757. His father was an itinerant Methodist preacher. By the age of twelve, Henderson was teaching Latin and Greek in Lady Huntington's college in Wales. He eventually became fluent in Persian, Arabic, Hebrew, Greek, Latin, Saxon, French, Spanish, Italian and German. Henderson wrote:

132

"If a parent send children into a wood wherein grow poisonous berries, and *certainly* knows they will eat of them, it is of no importance in the consideration of common sense, that he cautions, forbids, forewarns, or that they having *free will* may avoid the poison. Who will not accuse him of their death in sending them into circumstances where he *fore-knew* it would happen? God fore-knows every thing – to his knowledge every thing is certain."

"As, then, unceasing torments can answer no possible good to any one in the universe, I conclude them to be neither the will nor the work of God." (Whittemore, page 241, 243)

GEORGE MACDONALD: 1824 - 1905

A Scottish preacher, poet and novelist, George MacDonald was referred to by C.S. Lewis as his "master." His beliefs in Universalism are found throughout his writings. As an example:

"But at length, O God, wilt thou not cast Death and Hell into the lake of fire—even into thine own consuming self? Death shall then die everlastingly, and Hell itself will pass away, and leave her dolorous mansions to the peering day. Then indeed wilt thou be all in all. For then our poor brothers and sisters, every one – O God, we trust in thee, the Consuming Fire – shall have been burnt clean and brought home. For if their moans, myriads of ages away, would turn heaven for us into hell – shall a man be more merciful than God? Shall, of all his glories, his mercy alone not be infinite?" (From MacDonald's Unspoken Sermons Series One, "The Consuming Fire," pages 48-49...see Phillips, page 65.)

Elsewhere MacDonald writes:

"Punishment, I repeat, is not the thing required of God, but the absolute destruction of sin." (Phillips, page 73)

HANNAH WHITALL SMITH: 1832 - 1911

Best known for her classic "The Christian's Secret of a Happy Life" (1883), Hannah Whitall Smith also wrote a lesser known spiritual autobiography entitled "The Unselfishness of God and How I Discovered It." Originally published in 1903 by the Fleming H. Revell Company, this book has been republished more recently by Littlebrook Publishing in Princeton NJ. However, in republishing the work, the more recent version has omitted eight chapters, including references made to Smith's belief in universal reconciliation.

From Chapter 22, "The Third Epoch In My Religious Life (The Restitution of All Things),"

> "And I began to see that, since God had permitted sin to enter into the world, it must necessarily be that He would be compelled, in common fairness, to provide a remedy that would be equal to the disease. I remembered some mothers I had known, with children suffering from inherited diseases, who were only too thankful to lay down their lives in self-sacrifice for their children."

> "And with this a veil seemed to be withdrawn from before the plans of the universe, and I saw that it was true, as the Bible says, that 'as in Adam all die even so in Christ should all be made alive.' As was the first, even so was the second. The 'all' in one case could not in fairness mean less than the 'all' in the other. I saw therefore that the remedy must necessarily be equal to the disease, the salvation must be as universal as the fall."

> "And from that moment I have never had one questioning thought as to the final destiny of the human race."

> "There is to be a final 'restitution of all things' when, 'at the name of Jesus every knee shall bow, of things in heaven, and things on earth, and things under the earth, and every tongue shall confess that Jesus Christ is Lord to the glory of God the Father.' Every knee, every tongue – words could not be more

all embracing. The how and the when I could not see; but the one essential fact was all I needed – somewhere and somehow God was going to make everything right for all the creatures He had created."

"I hurried home to get hold of my Bible, to see if the magnificent fact I had discovered could possibly have been all this time in the Bible, and I not have seen it; and the moment I entered the house, I did not wait to take off my bonnet, but rushed at once to the table where I always kept my Bible and Concordance ready for use, and began my search. Immediately the whole Book seemed to be illuminated. On every page the truth concerning the 'times of restitution of all things,' of which the Apostle Peter says 'God hath spoken by the mouth of all His holy prophets since the world began,' shone forth, and no room was left for questioning."

From Chapter 23, "The Unselfishness of God,"

"How could a good God enjoy Himself in Heaven, knowing all the while that a large proportion of the beings He had Himself created were doomed to eternal misery, unless He were a selfish God?"

"But now I began to see that the wideness of God's love was far beyond any wideness that I could even conceive of."

"And if a person is a lost sinner, it only means that he is owned by the Good Shepherd, and that the Good Shepherd is bound, by the very duties of His ownership, to go after that which is lost, and to go until He finds it. The word 'lost' therefore, to my mind, contains in itself the strongest proof of ownership that one could desire. Who can imagine a mother with a lost child ever having a ray of comfort until the child is found, and who can imagine God being more indifferent than a mother?"

HANNAH HURNARD: 1905 - 1990

The author of the best selling "Hind's Feet on High Places" and "Mountains of Spices" says this in her lesser known book, "Unveiled Glory," written in 1956:

> "How could the Bible possibly speak of the perfect victory of God our Creator Who loves righteousness and cannot bear evil, if that victory really means that He cannot bring His own creatures at last to hate evil as He hates it, but must confirm multitudes, indeed the majority of them, in their choice of evil for ever and ever?"

> "The clearer these things presented themselves to my mind, the more plainly I saw that any supposed interpretation of the teaching of the Holy Scriptures which taught otherwise must be mistaken interpretations, because they are totally at variance to the revelation of a Holy God Who loves righteousness and hates evil, and Who only permits its existence temporarily that all creatures may learn to hate it and turn from it for ever."

> "I discovered that there is not one single verse in the Scriptures which uses the words everlasting, eternal, or forever and ever in connection with hell." (Quotations from pages 5-30 of "Unveiled Glory" by Hannah Hurnard.)

WILLIAM BARCLAY: 1907 - 1978

William Barclay devoted his entire life to the study of Scripture. Few, if any, knew the Greek language as well as Barclay.

In his autobiography entitled "A Spiritual Autobiography," Barclay writes:

> "But in one thing I would go beyond strict orthodoxy – I am a convinced universalist. I believe that in the end all men will be gathered into the love of God."

Barclay cites other believers in Universalism, including Origen and Gregory of Nyssa, but he goes on to delineate his own reasons for coming to a conclusion of universalism:

"First, there is the fact that there are things in the New Testament which more than justify this belief. Jesus said: 'I, when I am lifted up from the earth, will draw all men to myself.' (John 12:32) Paul writes to the Romans: 'God has consigned all men to disobedience, that he may have mercy on all.' (Romans 11:32) He writes to the Corinthians: 'As in Adam all die, so also in Christ shall all be made alive' (1 Corinthians 15:22); and he looks to the final total triumph when God will be everything to everyone. (1 Corinthians 15:28) In the First Letter to Timothy we read of God 'who desires all men to be saved and to come to the knowledge of the truth,' and of Christ Jesus 'who gave himself a ransom for all.' (1 Timothy 2:4-6) The New Testament itself is not in the least afraid of the word all.

"Second, one of the key passages is Matthew 25:46 where it is said that the rejected go away to ***eternal punishment***, and the righteous to eternal life. The Greek word for punishment is kolasis, which was not originally an ethical word at all. It originally meant the pruning of trees to make them grow better. I think it is true to say that in all Greek secular literature kolasis is never used of anything but remedial punishment. The word for eternal is aionios. The simplest way to put it is that aionios cannot be used properly of anyone but God; it is the word uniquely, as Plato saw it, of God. Eternal punishment is then literally that kind of remedial punishment which it befits God to give and which only God can give.

"Third, I believe that it is impossible to set limits to the grace of God. I believe that not only in this world, but in any other world there may be, the grace of God is still effective, still operative, still at work. I do not believe that the operation of the grace of God is limited to this world. I believe that the grace of God is as wide as the universe.

"Fourth, I believe implicitly in the ultimate and complete triumph of God, the time when all things will be subject to him, and when God will be everything to everyone. (1 Corinthians 15:24-28) For me this has certain consequences. If one man remains outside the love of God at the end of time, it means that that one man has defeated the love of God – and that is impossible. Further, there is only one way in which we can think of the triumph of God. If God was no more than a King or Judge, then it would be possible to speak of his triumph, if his enemies were still agonizing in hell or were totally and completely obliterated and wiped out. But God is not only King and Judge, God is Father – he is indeed Father more than anything else. No father could be happy while there were members of his family for ever in agony. No father would count it a triumph to obliterate the disobedient members of his family. The only triumph a father can know is to have all his family back home. The only victory love can enjoy is the day when its offer of love is answered by the return of love. The only possible final triumph is a universe loved by and in love with God." (From Chapter 3 of "A Spiritual Autobiography.")

OTHERS ACCEPTING THE DOCTRINE OF UNIVERSAL RECONCILIATION

Jukes writes in "Restitution of All Things,"

"Since the Reformation many of our English divines—among the Puritans Jeremiah White and Peter Sterry,—and in the English Church, Richard Clarke, William Law, and George Stonehouse,—in Scotland, Thomas Erskine of Linlathen and Bishop Ewing,—and among those on the Continent, Bengel, Oberlin, Hahn, and Tholuck,—have been believers in final restitution." (Jukes, pages 184, 187, 190)

Thomas Allin, in "Christ Triumphant" reports the following individuals who either openly taught or sympathized with Universalism:

> Tennyson, Browning and Mrs. Browning, Whitman, George MacDonald, Florence Nightingale, Emerson, Longfellow, Mrs. Beecher Stowe, Bishop Ewing of Argyll, Canon Kingsley, Bishop Westcott, F. W. Robertson, Phillips Brooks, Canon Farrar, Schleiermacher, Pastor Oberlin. (Allin, pages 166-7)

LESSONS FROM CHURCH HISTORY

1. As we have seen, a belief in an endless torment has not always been the dominant belief among Believers. Many, if not the majority of those within the early church, adhered to the doctrine of the ultimate reconciliation of all, including many of the most eminent "Church Fathers." We see also from the quotations of the "Church Fathers" that the doctrine of Universalism was based firmly upon the Scriptures.

2. By the time the Creeds were finally revised to include the doctrine of eternal punishment, those in power within "The Church" were motivated by politics, jealousy, and a narrowness of belief, even going so far as to execute those promoting "heretical" beliefs. Furthermore, Universalism was not officially condemned by the Church until the Fifth Council in 553 A.D., and was in harmony with the ancient Creeds.

3. One reason that the beliefs in universal reconciliation which existing in the early church are not better known is that many writings were destroyed when "The Church" determined they were heretical.

4. The primary opposition to Universalism in "ancient" church history came from the Latin Church, led by Augustine, where the Greek language was never mastered. In the centuries preceding

Augustine when Greek was the language of the "Church Fathers,"
Universalism appears to have been the majority view.

5. Perhaps the primary reason the orthodox church developed its
doctrine of eternal punishment stemmed from its fear that if
"eonian punishment" was not eternal, neither was "eonian life." It
was this **reasoning**, and not a close study of Scripture in its
original languages, that led to this doctrine. Had the leaders of
"orthodoxy" been able to see the "eonian" nature of God's
revelation, culminating with the consummation of the ages in 1
Corinthians 15, they would have seen that "eonian life" leads into
"eternity" at the end of the ages. There was, therefore, no real
threat to "eternal life," even though punishment/correction is not
eternal, but only for an age.

Chapter Ten

IF UNIVERSAL RECONCILIATION IS TRUE, WHY THE RESISTANCE?

If universal reconciliation is true, and if it is all so clear as I have made it seem in this study, why the resistance? Why are these things not more widely known?

During my own personal pilgrimage I asked these very questions. I had been raised within the church. I had studied my Bible. When I first encountered writings concerning the ultimate reconciliation of all I was very skeptical. The reality of an eternal hell was quite clear in my Bible, and I did not want to be led astray.

I had gone so far as to become an ordained pastor, first within the United Methodist Church where I served two small churches in southern Indiana for 3-1/2 years, and then within the Free Methodist Church where I served a church in central Kentucky for 5 years. As I preached, I continued to study and to ask questions. After much study and deliberation I came to the point where I could see in the Bible that it was ***possible*** that God would one day save all mankind, and I prayed that this was true. I continued to study, and to think for myself as I studied. I eventually reached the point where I became totally convinced that universal reconciliation was most definitely true.

At this point I began to search for a successor in the church I was serving, so as to provide a smooth transition. I did not feel it would be proper for me to remain within a church that adhered to a belief in an eternal hell, and I did not feel it would be proper for me to preach against this doctrine as it would create disunity and division. But this was a very difficult move for me. My wife and all of my five children, along with two daughters-in-law, had become a part of the church I served. What a wonderful thing to worship together as a family, and to be a part of the same church family. But it became very difficult to preach and to teach, because the ultimate salvation of all is found throughout all of God's Word if it is translated and interpreted correctly.

Furthermore, I had by this point become very convicted to share the truth of universal reconciliation openly. As the orthodox church proclaims a God of love who is willing to condemn many souls to an eternity in hell, I had come to see that God's character was being slandered. The church, for the most part, had become a false witness concerning God. "The Gospel" had become corrupted, and most leaders today preach and teach falsehoods.

It became clear to me that many individuals were driven away from God because of the falsehoods being proclaimed by the church. I think of my late father-in-law, Dr. Howard Maynard, who was a very intelligent man. He stayed out of churches for most of his adult life, unless he was in town for a visit, on which occasions he would attend our church. But I know from some of his questions and observations that he could see some serious problems with the gospel that was being proclaimed by the church. I wish I had been further down this path while he was still alive, so as to share these discussions with him.

When the Bible is translated so haphazardly and inconsistently, God's Word becomes distorted. The church has *created* a God Who is all wise and all powerful, but Who is *forced* to condemn most of His creation to an eternity in hell, despite the fact that it is His *will* that all mankind be saved. We have *created* a God of infinite love who is quite satisfied to look upon many of His creation burning forever in torment, even though many of these souls lived a better life when they had the chance than some who would be in heaven with Him.

But again, if universal reconciliation is so clearly taught in God's Word, why is it not more commonly proclaimed?

142

IT WILL PROMOTE SIN

"If all mankind will be saved, and if people know this is so, there is nothing to prevent them from sinning."

In other words, some would say that **"we need hell"** to hold the wicked in check. If they did not have hell to fear, the wicked would run rampant.

But look at the world in which we live! The threat of spending an eternity in hell, as it is commonly preached and taught today, has not restrained mankind! It seems that everyone persuades himself that he is not one of the wicked whose fate is hell.

Another problem is that there is such a great disproportion between eternal punishment and temporal human actions, so that few people who really think about the issue of eternal punishment really believe it is true. A punishment that is more proportioned to man's offences would be more believable, and more of a prevention against sin. And this is exactly what the Bible truly teaches...*temporal sin and evil resulting in a temporal suffering/discipline, with the purpose of restoring mankind in accord with the will of God.*

Furthermore, the real question is this..."Is there an eternal hell, or not?" If there is not (which the evidence provided in this book is intended to show), then we should not be proclaiming it, regardless of what we think the wicked in this world need!

WHAT ABOUT MISSIONS?

"If people believe in universal reconciliation they would not support missionaries."

First, let's not put the cart before the horse. Are we saying that even if universal reconciliation is true, we should preach the falsehood of an eternal torment so we do not adversely affect our missions program? Are we saying that we should perpetuate a falsehood (that God will send souls to hell forever) so that missionaries will have the motivation to carry on?

Missions, like any other type of preaching or teaching, should follow from the truth. Truth should not be altered, biased or suppressed to keep the missions program going.

WHY SHOULD WE PREACH AT ALL?

"If all mankind will eventually be saved, why bother preaching at all?"

Are we saying that our only motivation for preaching is to prevent people from going to hell? Paul preached and taught, and he did not ever mention hell. Isn't that interesting?

We proclaim the evangel because God instructs us to do so. We proclaim it because it is a wonderful truth. We proclaim it because we are God's Ambassadors, as if He is pleading through us. We proclaim it because we are dead to ourselves, and it is Christ who lives in us.

Once we come to understand that God is truly the Saviour of all mankind, telling others becomes even more of a joy. What an awesome God, who is wise enough to work through the ages to bring all mankind to the point of acceptance, despite the work of Satan and the evil devices of a rebellious mankind!

GOD IS HOLY AND CANNOT BEAR TO ALLOW SIN INTO HIS PRESENCE

This is the standard argument for the necessity of an eternal hell. "God is love and wants all mankind to be saved, but He is also holy and cannot put up with the presence of evil."

But we cannot say that evil must be evil forever. The wicked and rebellious are not incurable! It would be inconsistent with the character and wisdom of God to create a frail mankind with a propensity toward sin which is incurable.

In fact, God reveals to us in His Word the ultimate "cure" for *all mankind* at the end of the ages, made possible through the cross of Christ.

WHAT ADVANTAGE IS THERE IN BEING A CHRISTIAN?

"If all mankind will eventually be saved, what does it matter if one becomes a Christian in this lifetime?"

First, there is the lake of fire, the second death! Whether this is a very painful process, or simply death for a second time, we should want to spare all mankind from this fate.

Second, the Believer will enjoy life during the final eons when the non-Believer is in the lake of fire. This may be a very long time, and life during this time will be very worth living.

Third, once we become a Believer we enjoy, for the remainder of this lifetime, the *expectation* of the life to come. Even when we encounter the worst of experiences, our *expectation* cannot be taken from us.

Fourth, as Believers we are God's chosen witnesses in this lifetime. What a wonderful joy, not only to know God's plan for the ages, but to be able to share it as His Ambassadors.

Nathaniel Scarlett, who studied at Kingsford school under the patronage of John Wesley, and who published an improved translation of the New Testament in 1798, explains as follows:

> "The *saved* were those who were not to suffer punishment in the future life at all, while the *restored* were such as shall be delivered from it, after receiving judgment according to their works. Hence God is the *restorer* of all men, but the Saviour only of the elect, or first fruits, who are converted to him in this world." (From "The Modern History of Universalism," page 295.)

"DON'T TELL ME TOO MUCH...I DON'T WANT TO KNOW"

There are many comfortable Christians today who do not want things to change. There are families who have attended the same church for generations. There are individuals whose entire life is participation in a multitude of church activities.

I must be honest. I, too, was quite comfortable within the church. All of my children worshipped together. I was the pastor, and was looked to for leadership. I enjoyed being a part of this church family, doing my best to lead the people into a deeper study of God's Word and encouraging them to live their lives together as a true community, or family, of Believers.

I remember when I first began reading things concerning the ultimate salvation of all. At first I was very intrigued. Many questions began to clear up for me, and God's working through the ages made more sense. But there were times that I purposefully set aside these books, despite the truth that I saw within them, because I was not prepared to make a change. I was happy within the church, and I knew that if I went too far I would create disunity, arguments, and division.

But there came a time when I realized that truth is truth, and it is wrong to remain within a church that taught falsehoods concerning God. God is love. God is wise. God is all-powerful. I saw God's wonderful plan unfold in His Word (when properly translated and interpreted). God is truly in the process of bringing every single part of His creation into a willing subjection to Him. All will be saved at the end of the ages.

But I can sympathize with the many who know there is something to these teachings, but are not yet ready to take a stand, because they know there will be a price to be paid.

UPSETTING THE DOCTRINAL APPLE CART

I have worked for several large corporations, and it is very difficult to make changes. All possible side-effects must be examined before a move can be made because of the many and far-reaching implications.

If I had begun to preach universal reconciliation while I was still a pastor within the Free Methodist Church, there would have been quite a stir. I believe there are many within the ranks of Free Methodism, and any other mainstream Christian denomination, who either believe in universal reconciliation or who *would* believe if they heard the arguments and examined the evidence. I believe even some pastors and higher officials within the church believe these things. But if I had begun to preach in this way, pressure would have been exerted upon the officials to remove me. This would be necessary, because some people in the pews would create a stir or even leave the church.

The church has become an institution. We have taken what God's Word has to say about the Body of Christ, and we have turned it into an institution, with many of the same traits as a corporation. If people leave, giving decreases and bills cannot be paid. Churches own buildings with mortgage payments. Pastors must be paid, since for many this is their livelihood. Many pastors are financially precluded from preaching anything which might cost them their position, since they have large student loans to repay to their seminary, and families to support.

I'm not saying that pastors preach only for money, and that churches make their decisions based only on their finances. I am saying that these things exert a strong influence. Charles Pridgeon, founder of the Pittsburgh Bible Institute, writes in "Is Hell Eternal?"

> "Many a preacher has to wear a muzzle on certain questions or lose his church and his living." (page 19)

Fortunately I was a bi-vocational pastor, and I did not receive any compensation from the church I had served most recently. As coming

147

to the truth prompted me to leave, finances did not play a part in my decision. But I think of many of my seminary friends now serving churches, and I recognize the cost to them would be much greater.

Those who have been pastors for a significant length of time are looking at the pension they would be forfeiting. For them it would be easier to simply live within the system, and perhaps avoid preaching about hell. I don't believe God gave me that option.

Many pastors, teachers and professors have stood behind the concept of an eternal hell. One man once told me that hell was one of the "foundations of our faith." (I thought Jesus Christ was the only foundation of our faith!)

If leaders within the church suddenly began to preach and teach about universal reconciliation, there would most certainly be a price to pay. Theologies would need to be re-worked. Books would need to be retracted. Jobs would be lost and pensions forfeited. Attendance would drop, and bills would go unpaid. If the doctrinal apple cart were disrupted, this would be the state of affairs.

I think, though, if the many serious students of Scripture were faithful, orthodoxy could be turned around. Universal reconciliation was once a very popularly held belief in the early church. We've been off track since at least the 5th century A.D. in terms of the doctrine of hell. But it's not too late to recapture the truth.

LAZINESS
Some are simply too lazy to study God's Word in depth. They have been given their theology, either by their parents, teachers, pastors or professors...and they will go no further.

The masses will be forever satisfied with a simplified, easy to read translation of the Bible, despite the forfeiture of knowing truths God has chosen to reveal. This brings to mind 2 Timothy 4:3,

"For the era will be when they will not tolerate sound teaching, but their hearing being tickled, they will heap up for themselves teachers in accord with their own desires, and, indeed, they will be turning their hearing away from the truth, yet will be turned aside to myths."

TOO BUSY

Many in the world today are simply too busy to study the truths God has chosen to reveal to mankind. Some may even be busy doing the work of the church; the work they believe God has called them to. Some may even hear that there are biblical arguments supporting Universalism, but they are unwilling to set aside the things that are occupying their time to investigate this most important matter. In the meantime even as the many churches reach out to "the unchurched," God's character is tainted by a perverted "Gospel" because we are too busy to dig deeper and find the truth.

"I'M NOT SMART ENOUGH TO UNDERSTAND!"

Some will hear the basic arguments behind universal reconciliation, but they will simply say, "I'm not smart enough to understand these things." They will be content to live their life within the orthodox church, figuring that hell is not preached that often and they can live with it, even if they don't believe it. "After all," they might continue, "the church has many wonderful ministries and helps many people." This may be true, but I believe it is serious business to proclaim falsehoods about God, or to be a part of a church that represents God in this way. I believe it is time for people within the church to stand up against the system, to openly proclaim the full evangel.

Much has been written through the years in support of universal reconciliation, but most of what I have seen is very detailed and very scholarly. On the one hand I appreciate this. I can see that many who have preceded me have examined this issue from every possible angle, and they are convinced of the truth of universal reconciliation.

But many of these works are too in-depth and scholarly to be appreciated by the masses. Many will simply throw in the towel and concede defeat, thinking they have no alternative but to go along with the orthodox church, allowing the preachers and teachers to guide them.

I am writing for this very reason! I want to share with you the basic evidence in a simple way. This has not been easy. I want to show you enough of the facts so that you are not having to take my word for it, but I want to keep it simple enough to keep you thinking along with me. I hope I have succeeded. If I have, and if you wish to read more in depth on these things, I refer you to the list of books in the final chapter for further study.

SOME LIKE THE IDEA OF HELL
As hard as it is for me to understand, some people actually *like* the idea of hell. "After all, some people *deserve* to be there."

Jonathan Edwards and some of the hard core hell-fire preachers were able to convince their congregations that it would add to the pleasure of heaven to see the torment of the wicked. How wonderful to see Adolph Hitler or Osama bin Laden there.

But all of us are sinners! If God is able to take a man like Paul who killed the early Believers and did his best to wipe out the people of God, what are His limits?

And if it is even *possible* that God is willing and able to work through the ages to break the will of all mankind, reconciling Himself to every single one through the work of the cross, we should be praying our hearts out that this is His plan!

CHERISHED BELIEFS
Our religious beliefs become very solidly implanted, and we do not want to be led astray. This has some merit! We do want to stand solidly behind the truth, and want to be sure that we are not led astray.

But consider those of the Muslim faith! They cherish their beliefs. Consider those of the many Christian denominations, all clinging very strongly and faithfully to their beliefs. Consider the Mormons and the Jehovah Witnesses, who are very much off track in the eyes of most Christians. Consider those who believe that only the King James Version is the Word of God. We take some things very seriously, and we resist change. Sometimes we cannot even explain why we believe what we believe, but we cherish our beliefs nonetheless.

Upon hearing of my belief in universal reconciliation, a good friend told an acquaintance that I did not believe hell was eternal. Without even asking for details this acquaintance simply retorted, "Oh, it's eternal all right!"

In the first few centuries after Christ's departure we were led astray. Some beliefs were declared heretical, and most of the writings of those who fell into this category were destroyed. But was "The Church" correct in declaring these beliefs heretical? A review of church history quickly reveals that all of the "Church Fathers" were not driven by the purest of motives, and many believed that God's Word taught Universalism.

After considering the evidence presented in this book, I came to understand that "The Church" was wrong in some of its decisions, and the position in favor of an eternal hell falls into this category. Looking strictly to the Word of God, and not depending upon the traditions of "The Church," I have come to see that at the end of the ages, God will indeed save all mankind in accordance with His will!

"THE RESERVE DOCTRINE"

Some who understand that universal reconciliation is true, purposefully hold back in teaching the doctrine. The feeling is that the average person is not ready to hear these "professional secrets," so they are concealed by the teachers, preachers and scholars who have come to believe them.

151

This is the very reason for the Reformation. "The Church" had determined that God's Word should not be translated into a language that could be understood by the masses, since they would not understand and might even abuse the Word. Instead, "The Church" became the sole proprietor of God's Word, dispensing and teaching as it saw fit to the general public.

> "A great error of the Church has always been its assumption of authority over the souls of men in all matters of faith and dogma..." (From "The Ethnic Trinities" by Levi Paine, as reported in "Is Hell Eternal?" by Pridgeon.)

Paul uses the Greek word "musterion" several times in his writings. Many versions translate this word "mystery," but a better translation is "secret," since Paul clearly teaches that certain things *had been* kept secret by God in ages past, but were **now revealed**.

> "Thus let a man be reckoning with us – as deputies of Christ, and administrators of God's **secrets**." (1 Corinthians 4:1)

> "By revelation the **secret** is **made known to me** (according as I write before, in brief, by which you who are reading are able to apprehend my understanding in the **secret** of Christ, which, in other generations, is not made known to the sons of humanity as it was **now revealed** to His holy apostles and prophets..." (Ephesians 3:3ff)

> "To me, less than the least of all saints, was granted this grace: to bring the evangel of the untraceable riches of Christ to the nations, and to enlighten all as to what is the administration of the **secret**, which has been concealed from the eons in God, Who creates all, that **now may be made known** to the sovereignties and the authorities among the celestials, through the ecclesia, the multifarious wisdom of God, in accord with the purpose of the eons." (Ephesians 3:8ff)

So prior to Paul, there had been some things God had concealed, or kept secret, from mankind. But Paul tells us that to him certain secrets had been revealed by God. Once these things were revealed to

Paul, he proclaimed them and taught them. Paul saw no need to conceal them.

In "The Mystery of the Gospel" by A.E. Knoch we read:

> "The conclusion that there will be an actual, mutual, universal reconciliation is so astounding, so overwhelming, so glorious, that we cannot contain it; it must overflow." (page 199)

AFRAID TO BE LED ASTRAY

This is the *only* objection raised within this chapter that has real merit. The Bible warns us about false teachings and false prophets. We have been told our entire life that there is an eternal hell, and when we first hear that someone is teaching the salvation of all, we are skeptical. Well we should be! No one should be so easily swayed in his beliefs.

You believe in an eternal hell because you have always been taught this doctrine by those you have trusted. You believe it because you have trusted those who have given you the Bible translation you are using. Now I come along and am asking you to consider something contrary to those beliefs you have held for so long.

It is good for you to be skeptical, and I would not ask you to believe the things I believe simply because I am teaching them. But I am asking you to be like the Bereans, whom Paul described in Acts 17:11 as "more noble" because they did not simply listen to Paul, but they also examined the scriptures daily to see if Paul's teachings were true. The proper response is not to ignore the issue and to continue proclaiming a God Who is willing to condemn many to an eternal torment!

Consider the things I have presented in this work, and then search the Word of God for yourself.

THINK FOR YOURSELF!

As God's Ambassadors we must be faithful! If God has a plan to ultimately save all mankind, we should not be bearing false witness against Him by teaching about an eternal hell.

Hopefully I have caused you to re-think some things. This is a serious enough matter to warrant your study and consideration. It is not too difficult to understand. As you read what I have written, think for yourself. Look up the Scripture references along the way, and think! Don't be content to be trapped forever in your current belief system.

Chapter Eleven

HOW THEN SHALL WE LIVE?

As we study the Word of God our key question should always be, "How then shall we live?" Our study should not simply be intended to increase our knowledge. God has always, in every age, wanted His people to be a people of action.

Once we come to the conclusion that God will ultimately save all, does this knowledge change the way we are to live as a part of the Body of Christ?

I have always been intrigued by the debate between those believing we have absolute free will, and those taking the position of predestination. Both sides support their position with various Biblical texts. While the discussion has always been of some interest to me, the bottom line is that whatever position is correct, or if neither is correct, this doctrine does not change the way I am to live. Regardless, I am to live my life as God's Word directs me. I am to love others, help those in need, seek the will of God in my life, observe the various principles God has laid out for me in His Word (paying close attention to those behaviors God approves of, and those He does not), and proclaim the "Gospel" to others using the gifts God has given me.

Is it the same with the doctrine of universal reconciliation? If this doctrine does not ultimately change the way I am to live, why make such a big deal about it? Why rock the church boat? Why disturb Christians who are comfortable in their faith?

While I would say that for the most part our manner of life will not change once we come to the conclusion that God will ultimately save all, there is one major difference that cannot be overlooked! The Gospel that is being proclaimed throughout most of Christiandom is incorrect!

Paul defines our role in 2 Corinthians 5:20,

> "For Christ, then, are we ambassadors, as of God entreating through us. We are beseeching for Christ's sake, 'Be conciliated to God!' For the One not knowing sin, He makes to be a sin offering for our sakes that we may be becoming God's righteousness in Him."

Who are we? We are ambassadors! An ambassador is one who lives in a foreign country and represents his own country there. What message does an ambassador proclaim? Not his own, but the official message of his country. The ambassador is not there to set his own agenda, but to present the position of his country, which has been determined for him by the President and others in an official capacity.

We are God's ambassadors. Whose message are we proclaiming? Not our own message, but God's. The question is, *are we* proclaiming the correct message? If God reveals to us that it is His purpose, His will, and His intention to one day save all mankind, but if we proclaim that God will condemn many to an everlasting torment in hell, we are not being faithful ambassadors. We are not speaking God's message. Instead, we are proclaiming the message of "The Church," which I have found through a study of God's Word is much different than the message from God.

Consider the implications.

SLANDER & LIABLE
When someone teaches falsehood about another person, this is slander (or libel if these things are put into writing).

God has revealed to us that He will one day save all mankind. This is consistent with His vast love for His creation, and it shows us the great wisdom of God that He is able to bring all into subjection to Him, despite the rebellion and wickedness that currently permeates this world.

If we proclaim that God is willing to condemn many to an everlasting hell, we are slandering Him. We are teaching falsehoods about God. We are not serving Him as ambassadors, but are working against Him, proclaiming a message that is false.

Hannah Whitall Smith, in her original unedited "The Unselfishness of God" observes:

> "Still, to this day, the one thing which I find it very hard to tolerate, is anything which libels the character of God. Nothing else matters like this, for all our salvation depends wholly and entirely upon what God is…"

GOD'S CHARACTER
God has revealed to us that the most important principle is *LOVE!* All commandments are summed up in love. God is love.

Because we have been led astray by "The Church" and by incorrect Bible translations, we know that God is love but we are forced to reconcile this with the "fact" that many will be condemned to hell forever. We teach that while God is love, it is necessary that some are condemned to hell forever because God is holy and cannot bear the presence of sin.

So God must be portrayed in these two ways…as a God of love, and as a God of justice and holiness. God loves like a father, but He is OK with placing many of His creation into hell forever if they choose to reject Him in this short lifetime.

My point in this entire book has been to show you that *this is not the case.* God is love, God is holy and God is righteous and interested in justice. But as I have attempted to show in this work, all of these characteristics work together to accomplish God's ultimate purpose; the salvation of all mankind.

To proclaim that God is quite willing to cast many into an eternal torment is teaching something that is totally inconsistent with God's character.

KEEPING PEOPLE AWAY

With such an incorrect and inconsistent message that is being proclaimed, it is no wonder that many have stayed away from the faith. We must, to some extent, hold ourselves responsible for those who have rejected God.

Imagine being an unbeliever and hearing the message of the church for the first time.

"God loves you and wants to save you from your sins, so that you can live forever in heaven with Him. It's too bad this message got here too late for your other family members who never made a decision for Christ in this lifetime. That's the rules God has put into place. He does love us, but if we don't place our faith in Him in this lifetime He is forced to cast us into a fiery hell where we will be tormented, with no hope of relief, forever and ever. But not to worry, if you choose Christ this day you won't have to worry about that."

"Let me get this straight," says the world. "I live twenty years on this earth and I fail to understand who Christ is, even though I've been told about Him. I admit that I was in error. I can now see that. The problem is that I have died, and am now in hell, where I am being tormented, and where I will be kept alive forever and ever so that I can continue to be tormented. And now that I can see the error of my ways in that brief twenty year period I was given to live, it's too late to be forgiven and I will be spending all of eternity here in this awful place."

Sounds reasonable, doesn't it?

Is it any wonder that those of the world have a hard time understanding God as we have described Him? Where is the consistency in a God of superabounding love, Who commands us to love and forgive others for their offences, but Who is willing to cast many into a never ending hell, with no chance of forgiveness?

We are keeping people away from God when we proclaim a "gospel" like this. We're supposed to be ambassadors, but we don't know what we're talking about. We're representing God falsely, we're defaming His character, and we're driving people away from Him because of our inaccuracies.

IS THERE SUCH A BIG DIFFERENCE?
When it comes right down to it, we have been misled on a just few points by "The Church" since the 5th century.

There **is** a lake of fire. We can agree thus far. But on two points we disagree with what "The Church" has been teaching since the 5th century.

First, the lake of fire will not last forever and ever, but for the "eons of the eons." How long this period of time will be is up to God. But it is not endless. God's ultimate plan does not include a lake of fire. It exists to accomplish God's purposes, and we see God's purposes being finally accomplished in 1 Corinthians 15, whereupon the lake of fire (death) is abolished.

Second, the purpose of the lake of fire is not to torment endlessly as a punishment, but it is to refine, to discipline, to correct, to purge, and to bring those within it to the point where every knee bows and every tongue confesses that Jesus Christ is Lord, to the glory of God.

While the lake of fire is not endless, it is certainly not a place we would want any man or woman to be cast into. We have great incentive to proclaim the *message for today* that has been entrusted to us as ambassadors:

"Be conciliated to God! For the One not knowing sin, He makes to be a sin offering for our sakes that we may be becoming God's righteousness in Him."
(2 Corinthians 5:21)

The difference seems so small. We only vary on two points...the duration of the lake of fire, and its purpose.

But these two points make all the difference in the world as it relates to how we represent the character of God.

WE ARE NOT QUESTIONING GOD

I want to make it very clear that nothing in this work should be seen as questioning God. If God said that there was an endless torment, I would certainly believe Him. He is the creator of this universe, and He has the absolute right to set the rules as He sees fit.

But God has revealed to mankind that this is not the case, as I have done my best to show throughout this work.

I would not question God. I am questioning those who have inconsistently, erroneously and carelessly translated His Word, distorting it to fit the biases and teachings of man.

Seek the pure Word of God. Think about the things I have presented in this work. Question those who teach you otherwise. Study, think and pray!

AT THE VERY LEAST...

Having been exposed to the things I have presented in this work, at the very least you should be hoping and praying that these things are true.

Not wanting to be led astray, this is where I began. I had been taught my entire life that there was a place of eternal torment. When I first heard of the possibility that this was wrong, I was highly skeptical. I did not want to be led into falsehood.

But as I journeyed down the path, studying and thinking of these things I had never been taught by a teacher or a pastor, I came first to a place where I did not know if these things were true, but I certainly hoped and prayed that they were!

How can we not feel this way? To think that there really is hope for those of our loved ones who died outside of Christ! Can God's grace really be that big? Can His love really go that far? Is He really that wise that He could figure out a way to save all of mankind, despite rebellion and sin and wickedness and rejection?

This is a good place to start. The things you have read in this book have been largely suppressed, at least since the 5th century. When Universalism was declared by "The Church" to be heresy, many of the writings in support of this doctrine were destroyed. "The Church" was wrong, and today we live with the results of that error.

At least begin by hoping and praying that these things are true. Read and study the Word of God with this new possibility; this new perspective. Test this theory, this theology. Don't believe me, but study and think for yourself.

I think as you go forward you will see the wonderful grace of God at every turn. It is a grace that is greater than anything mankind could ever have hoped for!

Chapter Twelve

A SUMMARY OF THE FACTS IN SUPPORT OF UNIVERSAL RECONCILIATION

Let us take a few minutes to quickly review the facts in support of the doctrine of universal reconciliation.

ETERNAL, OR EONIAN?

The word commonly translated "eternal" (aionian) in our modern Bible translations should be "eonian" or "age-abiding."

  a. This is clear from within God's Word itself, when examining the various forms of the word used (plural, before the eons, after the eons, etc).

  b. This was the common understanding of those within the church in the first few centuries following the departure of Christ.

The implication is that punishment/correction is not eternal, but for an age (however long God determines is necessary to accomplish His purpose).

ALL, OR SOME?

There are many passages throughout God's Word that speak of *ALL* being saved, just as *ALL* died in Adam.

a. It is clearly God's **will** that all are saved. (1 Timothy 2:4)

b. God operates all in accord with the counsel of His will. (Ephesians 1:11)

We have had difficulties with these *ALL* passages because of the many other passages that seem to be talking about **some** spending eternity in hell. But once we see that punishment/correction is not endless, but is for a period of time, we can understand how ultimately *ALL* will be saved.

HELL

The word commonly translated "hell" in our modern Bible translations is totally incorrect, as it is a combining of:

a. The Hebrew "sheol" (unseen place)

b. The Greek "hades" (unseen place)

c. The Greek "Gehenna" (the Valley of Hinnom, a physical refuse dump outside of Jerusalem where those guilty of certain crimes in the physical earthly kingdom will be cast)

d. The Greek "Tartarus" (a holding place for angels, not human beings, as they await judgment)

Hell is not spoken of anywhere in the entire Old Testament. The penalty for sin is **death**, and death (destruction) is the sole penalty we see meted out in the Old Testament. Likewise, Paul has much to say about Christian living, but does not teach of an eternal torment for those outside the Body of Christ. The passages which are primarily found within the four Gospels (Matthew, Mark, Luke, John) that talk of punishment are referring to punishment in the kingdom to come upon the earth when Christ returns. We see this physical, earthly kingdom become a reality in the book of Revelation.

Our notion of "hell" comes from pagan writers who developed fictional speculations about the afterlife. As for the Hebrew and Greek words which are translated "hell" in our modern translations, a careful study will show that none speak of the "hell" that "The Church" teaches about.

LAKE OF FIRE

The "Lake of Fire" is,

    a. Not eternal, but will be "abolished" at the end of the ages, and

    b. Not for the purpose of tormenting, but to refine, purge, and correct.

Temporal wickedness and rejection of God in this life is compensated with a temporal (and not eternal) punishment/correction, with the ultimate purpose of restoring all of God's creation. This is consistent with God's character of love; a loving Father who will not be satisfied until the final lost sheep is safely within the fold.

THE CONSUMMATION

Revelation tells us of things which will take place in the final eons (ages).

1 Corinthians 15 tells us of things which will take place after the eons (ages) have concluded. Here we see the climax of God's revelation, when all things (mankind included) come into a willing subjection to Christ, and when God becomes All in all.

We cannot confuse the end of Revelation (the final eon) where the lake of fire is still burning, with 1 Corinthians 15 (after the eons have concluded) where the lake of fire (death) is abolished and all things are now reconciled to God.

Chapter Thirteen

WHAT TO DO NEXT?

This book is not intended to be an exhaustive study of every point raised. It is a look at the basics. But where do we go from here? Following are a few suggestions.

1. Purchase a copy of the Concordant Literal New Testament and begin using it alongside the version you have used in the past. Get the hard bound edition which includes the Keyword Concordance, allowing you to study the uses of various words used in the original manuscripts. If you are interested in much deeper scriptural studies, subscribe to "Unsearchable Riches" magazine, also available from Concordant Publishing, and ask for a list of books available.

    Concordant Publishing Concern
    15570 Knochaven Road
    Santa Clarita, CA 91350
    661/252-2112
    email@concordant.org

2. Read this book a second time after you have your Concordant Literal New Testament, looking up each reference being referred to, and examining the entire context.

3. Think about the principles brought forth in this book as you continue to study God's Word. Test the theories (theologies) which have been presented.

4. As you attend Bible studies where ideas are raised that are not consistent with what you have come to see is true, don't be afraid to ask questions and share your ideas. Don't do this with an attitude that you know more than others, or that you are trying to cause friction. But don't remain silent as things are being taught which are not correct.

5. If you are interested in getting involved in a Bible study with others of like mind in the matter of universal reconciliation, write to me and I will attempt to link you with fellowships that meet in your area. You can write to me at:

    Grace Evangel Fellowship
    P. O. Box 6
    Wilmore, KY 40390
    bobevely@juno.com

6. Many of the books written on this subject matter are very deep and scholarly. The goal of Grace Evangel Fellowship is to teach things in a way that the average person is able to understand. It is wonderful if you are led to a desire to study in a deeper way, but our intent is to teach the basics, showing you where you can find materials if you desire to dig deeper. Basic workshops are held at various locations, and a newsletter is available. Inquire to Grace Evangel Fellowship at the address or e-mail listed above.

Visit us at www.graceevangel.org

Chapter Fourteen

RECOMMENDED READING

The following are recommended reading for those wishing to learn more about God's plan for the ages.

THE CONCORDANT VERSION, & STUDY HELPS

"The Concordant Literal New Testament With Keyword Concordance"
Concordant Publishing Concern
15570 Knochaven Road, Santa Clarita, CA 91387
661/252-2112   email@concordant.org
www.concordant.org
This is by far the best translation of the New Testament available; not easy to read, but very accurate and very consistent. The Keyword Concordance in the back of the volume will allow you to search other occurrences of the same Greek word.
[The Concordant Literal New Testament is also available on CD ROM.]

"The Concordant Version of the Old Testament"
Concordant Publishing Concern
[Not entirely completed, but many of the individual books in the Old Testament can be purchased from the publisher.]

"Unsearchable Riches" – a bimonthly magazine

167

Concordant Publishing Concern
[A wonderful magazine filled with thought-provoking and well researched articles concerning the Word of God. All back issues are still available since the magazine was first published in 1909, and a topical and text index is also available from the publisher.]

The Englishman's Greek Concordance
George V. Wigram, First published in 1839.
Baker Book House, Grand Rapids, M, 1979.
(Numerically coded to Strong's Exhaustive Concordance.) This reference book allows you to easily search every occurrence of any Greek word in the New Testament, and you don't need to know Greek to use it.

GENERAL

Christ Triumphant
Thomas Allin, 1890.
Reprinted by Concordant Publishing Concern.

Christ Victorious Over All
Joseph S. Johnston
Self Published, 1921.

God's Eonian Purpose
Adlai Loudy, ConcordantPublishing Concern
Contains great summaries of church history and the word "eonian"

God's Truths Recovered
Daniel Russino, 1992.
DeSans Publications, Verona PA. 15147.

Is Hell Eternal, or, Will God's Plan Fail?
Rev. Charles H. Pridgeon, 1931.
The Evangelization Society of The Pittsburgh Bible Institute.

The Mystery of the Gospel
A. E. Knoch
Concordant Publishing Concern. 1969.
[Good overview of God's plan through the ages. Pages 199-262 go into a detailed study of "eonian."]

Restitution of All Things
Andrew Jukes, 1867.
Republished by Concordant Publishing Concern.

Salvator Mundi: or, Is Christ the Saviour of All Men?
Samuel Cox
Kegan Paul, Trench & Co, London. 1888.
Republished by Saviour of All Fellowship, 6800 Hough Rd, Almont MI 48003.
www.saviour-of-all.org

Universal Reconciliation, A Brief Selection of Pertinent Quotations
Compiled and introduced by Michael Phillips
Sunrise Books, Eureka CA.

The Unselfishness of God, and How I Discovered It
Hannah Whitall Smith, 1903.
Fleming H. Revell Company, London and Edinburgh.
(Look for the original, now out of print version, and not the newer edited version.)

CHURCH HISTORY

The Ancient History of Universalism
Hosea Ballou, 1829.
Republished by Saviour of All Fellowship, 6800 Hough Rd, Almont MI 48003.

The Modern History of Universalism
Thomas Whittemore, 1830.
Republished by Saviour of All Fellowship, 6800 Hough Rd, Almont MI 48003.

EONIAN

Eonian, Everlasting or Age Lasting?
Compiled by Grace H. Todd with Appendixes by Joseph E. Kirk.
Concordant Publishing Concern.

The Greek Word Aion-Aionios, Translated Everlasting-Eternal, in the Holy Bible, Shown To Denote Limited Duration.
Rev. John Wesley Hanson, 1875.
Reprinted 1995 by Saviour of All Fellowship, 6800 Hough Rd, Almont MI 48003.

Whence Eternity?
Alexander Thomson.
Concordant Publishing Concern.

HELL & JUDGMENT

God's Truths Recovered *by Daniel Russino*
DeSans Publications, Verona PA 15147 (reference chapter 9)

Universal Reconciliation, A Brief Selection of Pertinent Quotations
Compiled and introduced by Michael Phillips.
Sunrise Books, Eureka CA. 1998.

IS THE BIBLE REALLY THE WORD OF GOD?

God's Eonian Purpose

Adlai Loudy, Concordant Publishing Concern
15570 Knochaven Road, Santa Clarita, CA 91387
661/252-2112   email@concordant.org
www.concordant.org
[A good synopsis in Chapters 1 and 2.]

Know Why You Believe

Paul Little, InterVarsity Press
[Easy to read with good information. Not as detailed as McDowell's book.]

The New Evidence That Demands a Verdict

Josh McDowell, Thomas Nelson Publishers
[Very detailed and well organized.]

ABOUT THE AUTHOR

Bob Evely is a national Marketing Manager for a real estate information company. He is a graduate of Oakland University (Rochester, Michigan) and has an M.Div. degree from Asbury Theological Seminary (Wilmore, Kentucky). For three and a half years Bob served as pastor of the Canton and West Point United Methodist Churches in Salem, Indiana; and then for five years he served as pastor of the Open Door Free Methodist Church in Nicholasville, Kentucky. Both were bi-vocational positions, with Bob supporting his family through his full time employment.

In May, 2002 Bob resigned as pastor of Open Door Free Methodist Church to found Grace Evangel Fellowship, a home church based in Wilmore, Kentucky. The Evelys plan to grow this ministry into multiple home church fellowships that will occasionally meet together as a larger body.

Bob resides in Wilmore, Kentucky with his wife Jill. Originally from the Romeo, Michigan area, the Evelys have been married for 27 years and have five children: Cris (and wife Jen) of Lexington, Kentucky; Dusty (and wife Sharon) of Wilmore, Kentucky; and Chad (20), Kari (16) and Scott (13) still at home in Wilmore. Jill has homeschooled all five children through the 9th grade, with Scott still being educated at home. Jill also represents a literature based homeschool curriculum, as a consultant.

This is the first book by the author. He can be contacted by writing to Grace Evangel Fellowship, P. O. Box 6, Wilmore, Kentucky 40390.

Printed in the United States
16029LVS00007B/1-78